# 200 make ahead dishes

# hamlyn | **all colour cookbook**

# 200 make ahead dishes

Sara Lewis

An Hachette Livre UK Ltd
www.hachettelivre.co.uk

First published in Great Britain in 2008 by Hamlyn,
a division of Octopus Publishing Group Ltd,
2–4 Heron Quays, London E14 4JP

ISBN 978-0-600-61820-1

A CIP catalogue record for this book is available from the
British Library.

Printed and bound in China

10 9 8 7 6 5 4 3 2 1

For Rosalind, wonderfully hospitable but
a very last-minute cook. Perhaps this will help!

Both metric and imperial measurements have been given
in all recipes. Use one set of measurements only, and not
a mixture of both.

Standard level spoon measurements are used in all recipes.
1 tablespoon = one 15 ml spoon
1 teaspoon = one 5 ml spoon

Ovens should be preheated to the specified temperature
– if using a fan-assisted oven, follow the manufacturer's
instructions for adjusting the time and the temperature.

Fresh herbs should be used unless otherwise stated.

Medium eggs should be used unless otherwise stated.

The Department of Health advises that eggs should not be
consumed raw. This book contains some dishes made with
raw or lightly cooked eggs. It is prudent for vulnerable
people such as pregnant and nursing mothers, invalids, the
elderly, babies and young children to avoid uncooked or
lightly cooked dishes made with eggs. Once prepared, these
dishes should be kept refrigerated and used promptly.

This book includes dishes made with nuts and nut
derivatives. It is advisable for those with known allergic
reactions to nuts and nut derivatives and those who may be
potentially vulnerable to these allergies, such as pregnant and
nursing mothers, invalids, the elderly, babies and children, to
avoid dishes made with nuts and nut oils. It is also prudent to
check the labels of pre-prepared ingredients for the possible
inclusion of nut derivatives.

Finishing time refers to how long it will take you to complete
the dish when ready to serve.

# contents

# introduction

# introduction

We all lead such busy lives nowadays that any method for reducing stress should be welcomed. Finding time to make a healthy and enjoyable meal for the family, or something special for friends, can sometimes feel like another chore, but it needn't be. Making food in advance ready to bake later in the day may sound a little old fashioned, but don't discount it.

While no one is suggesting that you knock up a fish pie before getting the 8.03 train to work, part-making dishes at the weekend leaves you free to indulge in a little retail therapy, a trip to the gym or a long walk with the dog. Then when you return you can sit

down and relax with a drink while supper reheats, filling the house with all its wonderful aromas.

Making food to share with friends is also much more relaxing when you have done most of the work earlier in the day. When your guests arrive you can enjoy their company, rather than spending all your time in the kitchen.

For those with young families, supper can be started while very young children have a morning nap or are at school, then when you feel at your most tired you have time for a cuddle and a story while supper cooks. If you work shifts, making food earlier in the day, or even the evening before, is also a boon as supper can be left with a note so that the first home pops it in the oven, ready for everyone to tuck into the minute they walk in.

If you are newly retired, it can be liberating to make supper early in the day then go out and enjoy your long-awaited free time and eat whenever you feel like it, so maximizing your time on the golf course or in pursuit of new hobbies. Or why not go out for the day with a gourmet picnic lunch, such as a raised pork and chicken Picnic Pie, or Pan Bagna.

This book contains an eclectic selection of traditional and modern recipes, with something to suit all moods and occasions, to help you get one step ahead.

# make ahead hints & tips

## be organized
The key to success when it comes to making meals in advance is to be organized. Plan what you are going to eat well in advance so you know which ingredients you need to buy, what you need to prepare and when. If you have to, write it down so you don't forget.

## choose the right dishes
Some dishes lend themselves to being made in advance. Moist dishes that cook for a long time, such as curries, casseroles and soups, are often even better when made in advance and reheated as the flavours get a chance to really develop. Or choose mousses, salads, sushi or desserts which are served cold and can be kept chilled until you want to eat them. With these dishes you have nothing at all to do just before serving, making them perfect for entertaining. Other dishes, such as pies or kebabs, can be part-made in advance, then simply baked or grilled at the last minute.

## frozen assets
It may sound a little old fashioned, but the freezer can be a great help to the busy cook. A few well-chosen supplies can be quickly transformed into an easy dessert. Frozen fruits such as raspberries, blackberries, blueberries and cranberries look just as good

when defrosted as fresh and make pretty accompaniments to desserts such as crème caramel or even a good-quality ice cream, or as the base for a warming crumble. Packs of frozen puff, shortcrust and filo pastry save greatly on time and effort – think sweet as well as savoury pies. Don't throw those stale bits of bread away, but make into crumbs and freeze ready for sprinkling on to cheesy gratin dishes or mixing into stuffings.

## get planting
Don't forget a few pots of fresh herbs by the front or back door. Herbs not only look pretty but can save money too and mean that you always have a handy supply for a garnish or extra flavour whenever you need it.

# food hygiene

When cooking meals in advance, food hygiene becomes extremely important. If food is wrongly stored, handled or reheated, harmful bacteria can multiply and eventually cause food poisoning. Follow these simple guidelines to make sure your food is safe.

## cover ups

Once food is prepared and ready to be set aside for later it is important to cover dishes to prevent food from drying out. Use either kitchen foil, clingfilm or, if chilling in the dish it was cooked in, the casserole or saucepan lid. Choose kitchen foil or the dish lid if the food will be reheated, covered, in the oven. Use clingfilm for salads or oven-baked dishes that are cooked uncovered for a golden crust.

## cooling

Once food has been cooked, cover it and leave it to cool to room temperature. As soon as it is cool enough, transfer it to the refrigerator until required.

Speed up the cooling of meat dishes such as casseroles or pâtés by standing the covered cooking dish in a sink or roasting tin filled with cold water.

## refrigerator reminders

• The bottom of the refrigerator is the coldest part as cold air falls.
• Always cover food, either raw or cooked, before putting it in the refrigerator. This not only prevents food from drying out but also helps to prevent strong flavours, particularly garlicky or spicy ones, from transferring.
• Keep cooked and uncooked foods on separate shelves to prevent contamination, with uncooked foods on the lower shelves.
• Make sure that meat or fish juices – which are high in bacteria – cannot drip on to other foods, particularly those that will be eaten raw such as salad or cheese.
• Never put warm dishes in the refrigerator.
• Do not overcrowd the refrigerator or the cold air will not be able to circulate freely.
• Keep the times that the refrigerator door is open to a minimum to maintain a safe temperature and save energy.

## listeria

There is only a small risk of a healthy person contracting listeriosis. It is recommended that those most at risk, such as the elderly, pregnant mothers or those recovering from illness, avoid foods which have been found to contain high levels of listeria bacteria as these can continue to multiply at refrigerator temperatures. These foods include soft mould-ripened cheeses such as Brie, Camembert and blue cheeses; meat, fish or vegetable pâtés; and raw unpasteurized milk and milk products.

## what temperature?

Refrigerators should be kept at a temperature of 0–5°C (32–41°F) in the centre to the lower shelves. You can buy a refrigerator thermometer from a hardware or kitchen shop. You may need to reduce the temperature during summer.

## reheating

Correct reheating of make ahead meals is as important as correct storage. There are three golden rules:
• Only reheat foods once.
• If you don't require the full amount reheated, then take a portion out and reheat so that the remaining portions may be reheated later.
• Always make sure that the food is piping hot right through before serving.

## reheating on the hob

Make sure that food is brought to boiling point and then kept at that temperature for 5 minutes, stirring to make sure that it does not stick to the base of the pan.

## reheating in the oven

Reheat food at 180°C (350°F), Gas Mark 4, or above for a minimum of 20 minutes or for longer if a large dish, until piping hot right through.

## reheating in the microwave

Do not use metal dishes to reheat in the microwave, and beware of china dishes that have metal decoration as these will cause sparks while the microwave is in operation. Everyday china plates and bowls are fine, but be wary of pottery dishes as these can get as hot as the food, so use a cloth to remove items from the microwave.

Cover food with clingfilm while reheating to prevent it from splattering all over the microwave interior. Pierce the film once or twice to allow the steam to escape.

Reheat dishes thoroughly, rather than to the point that it is just hot enough to eat. Food must be heated until piping hot throughout, ideally held at 70°C (158°F) for 2 minutes.

Always stir foods before serving to disperse any hot spots.

# starters

# smoked salmon & prawn sushi

Preparation time **40 minutes**
Cooking time **20–25 minutes**
Finishing time **5 minutes**
Serves **4–6**

450 ml (¾ pint) **water**
250 g (8 oz) sushi **rice**
4 tablespoons rice **vinegar**
1 teaspoon **wasabi paste**,
  plus extra to serve
250 g (8 oz) cooked **tiger
  prawns**
grated rind and juice of
  2 **limes**
5 sheets **nori seaweed**
200 g (7 oz) sliced **smoked
  salmon**
40 g (1½ oz) bottled Japanese
  **ginger**, drained
325 g (11 oz) jar of red
  **pimentos**, drained and cut
  into long strips
3 **spring onions**, cut into long
  thin strips

**Bring** the water to the boil in a saucepan, add the rice, cover and simmer gently for 20–25 minutes until very soft. Drain off any excess water. Mix the vinegar and wasabi and stir into the rice. Leave to cool. Toss the prawns with the lime rind and juice and set aside.

**Place** one nori sheet on a bamboo rolling mat, spoon over one-fifth of the rice and spread into an even layer, leaving a small border of nori showing. Arrange one-fifth of the smoked salmon in a long line in the centre of the rice. Next to that add one-fifth of the prawns, and on top some ginger, pimentos and spring onions.

**Using** the mat to help, roll up the nori sheet so the rice wraps around the filling and the edges of nori overlap slightly. Rock back and forth for an even shape. Repeat to make the remaining rolls. Wrap them individually in clingfilm and chill until required.

**When** ready to serve, cut the rolls into thick slices and arrange with cut edges uppermost on a plate. Serve with extra wasabi.

**For fennel & asparagus sushi**, cut a fennel bulb into strips and blanch in boiling water with 150 g (5 oz) asparagus for 2 minutes until just tender. Refresh the vegetables in cold water, then drain and pat dry with kitchen paper. Use the fennel and asparagus in place of the smoked salmon and prawns.

# cherry tomato tarts with pesto

Preparation time **15 minutes**
Finishing time **18 minutes**
Serves **4**

375 g (12 oz) cherry
  **tomatoes**
2 tablespoons **olive oil**
1 **onion**, finely chopped
2 **garlic** cloves, crushed
3 tablespoons **sun-dried**
  **tomato paste**
325 g (11 oz) ready-made
  **puff pastry**
beaten **egg**, to glaze
150 g (5 oz) **crème fraîche**
2 tablespoons **pesto**
**salt** and **pepper**

**Lightly** grease a large baking sheet and sprinkle with water. Halve about 150 g (5 oz) of the tomatoes. Heat the oil in a frying pan, add the onion and fry for about 3 minutes until softened. Remove the pan from the heat, add the garlic and sun-dried tomato paste, then stir in all the tomatoes, turning until they are lightly coated in the sauce. Chill and set aside until required.

**Roll** out the pastry on a lightly floured surface and cut out four 12 cm (5 inch) rounds using a cutter or small bowl as a guide. Transfer to the prepared baking sheet and make a shallow cut 1 cm (½ inch) in from the edge of each round using the tip of a sharp knife, to form a rim. Brush the rims with beaten egg. Cover, chill and set aside until required.

**Lightly** mix together the crème fraîche, pesto and salt and pepper in a bowl so that the crème fraîche is streaked with the pesto. Cover, chill and set aside until required.

**When** ready to serve, pile the tomato mixture on to the centres of the pastries, making sure the mixture stays within the rims. Bake the tartlets in a preheated oven, 220°C (425°F), Gas Mark 7, for about 15 minutes until the pastry is risen and golden. Transfer the tartlets to serving plates and spoon the crème fraîche and pesto mixture into a small serving dish. Serve scattered with basil leaves.

**For homemade pesto**, put 1 chopped garlic clove, a large handful of basil leaves, 3 tablespoons pine nuts and 50 g (2 oz) grated Parmesan cheese in a food processor or blender and process, gradually adding a little olive oil to make a thick, oily paste.

# gravadlax with dill sauce

Preparation time **10 minutes**,
plus **2–3 days** marinating
Finishing time **15 minutes**
Serves **4–6**

large handful of **dill**
1 tablespoon **mixed
   peppercorns**, roughly
   crushed
2 tablespoons **salt flakes**
2 tablespoons golden caster
   or light muscovado **sugar**
500 g (1 lb) piece of thick
   **salmon** fillet, skinned

**Dill sauce**
2 tablespoons Swedish or
   Dijon **mustard**
4 teaspoons golden caster or
   light muscovado **sugar**
3 tablespoons sunflower **oil**
1–2 teaspoons white wine
   **vinegar**
2 tablespoons chopped **dill**
**pepper**

**Tear** half the dill into pieces on to a plate. Add the peppercorns, salt and sugar and mix together. Coat both sides of the salmon in the dill mixture then transfer to a large strong plastic bag with any mixture from the plate. Seal the bag and stand in a shallow dish. Cover with a chopping board and weigh down with an unopened bag of flour, bags of sugar or cans. Marinate in the refrigerator for 2–3 days, turning twice a day.

**On** the day of serving, make the sauce by mixing the mustard and sugar together in a small bowl. Gradually trickle in the oil, little by little, whisking continuously until thickened. Thin the sauce with vinegar to taste. Stir in the chopped dill and season with pepper.

**When** ready to serve, lift the salmon out of the marinade, drain, put on a chopping board. Sprinkle with the remaining dill, torn into pieces. Cut into thin slices with the knife at a 45 degree angle to the fish. Arrange on serving plates with spoonfuls of the sauce and a little salad garnish. Serve with brown bread.

**For honeyed gravadlax with fennel & dill**, add 1 teaspoon roughly crushed fennel seeds to the marinade mixture, and use 2 tablespoons thick set honey instead of the sugar. Serve in the same way, accompanied by dill sauce and brown bread.

# spring rolls

Preparation time **20 minutes**,
plus soaking
Finishing time **about
40 minutes**
Makes **40**

50 g (2 oz) thin cellophane
(bean thread) **noodles**
15 g (½ oz) dried **black ear
fungus**
125 g (4 oz) minced **pork**
2 **shallots**, chopped
3 **garlic** cloves, crushed
2.5 cm (1 inch) piece of fresh
root **ginger**, peeled and
finely chopped
½ tablespoon **soy sauce**
10 round **rice papers**
2 **eggs**, beaten
groundnut **oil**, for deep-frying
ground black **pepper**

**Soak** the noodles and fungus in separate bowls of
warm water for 20 minutes or until they are soft.

**Use** scissors to snip the noodles into 2.5 cm (1 inch)
lengths and chop the fungus into small pieces. Mix
together with the pork, shallots, garlic, ginger, soy
sauce and pepper.

**Cut** each round of rice paper into 4 quarters. Brush
each quarter with egg and leave to soften for a couple
of minutes. Place 1 heaped teaspoon of filling towards
the rounded edge of the rice paper, fold in the sides
and roll up towards the pointed end. Repeat with the
remaining filling and rice paper. Cover and chill the rolls
until required.

**When** ready to serve, heat the oil for deep-frying in a
saucepan until a cube of bread browns in 2 minutes.
Add about 6 spring rolls and cook for 6–8 minutes or
until they are golden brown and the filling cooked
through. Repeat with the remaining spring rolls and
serve immediately with sweet chilli dipping sauce.

**For prawn spring rolls**, prepare the noodles, garlic
and ginger as above. Mix with 75 g (3 oz) bean
sprouts, 1 small grated carrot, 3 sliced spring onions,
2 tablespoons chopped fresh coriander, 150 g (5 oz)
cooked peeled prawns and 2 teaspoons Thai fish
sauce. Separate the rice papers but leave whole.
Brush with egg, divide the filling between them, then
fold in the sides and roll up. Cook as above.

# chickpea & parsley soup

Preparation time **15 minutes**, plus soaking
Cooking time **1½–2 hours**
Finishing time **5 minutes**
Serves **4–6**

250 g (8 oz) dried **chickpeas**, soaked overnight
1 small **onion**, quartered
3 **garlic** cloves
40 g (1½ oz) **parsley**
2 tablespoons **olive oil**
1.2 litres (2 pints) **vegetable stock**
finely grated rind and juice of ½ **lemon**
**salt** and **pepper**

**Drain** the chickpeas, rinse in cold water and drain again. Put them in a saucepan of fresh water, bring to the boil, boil rapidly for 10 minutes then simmer for 1–1½ hours, until just tender.

**Put** the onion, garlic and parsley in a food processor or blender and blend until finely chopped. Heat the oil in a large saucepan and cook the onion mixture over a low heat until slightly softened.

**Add** the chickpeas and cook gently for 1–2 minutes. Add the stock, season well with salt and pepper and bring to the boil. Cover and cook for 20 minutes, or until the chickpeas are really tender.

**Allow** the soup to cool a little, then part-purée it in a food processor or blender, or mash it with a fork, so that it retains plenty of texture. Cover and chill until required.

**When** ready to serve, pour the soup into a clean pan, add the lemon juice, adjust the seasoning as necessary and heat through. Serve the soup topped with grated lemon rind and cracked black pepper.

**For lentil & coriander soup**, cook 250 g (8 oz) red lentils in a covered saucepan with 1 litre (1¾ pints) gently simmering water for 30 minutes until just tender. Process 1 onion, 1 large mild deseeded red chilli, 3 garlic cloves, 1 tablespoon curry paste and 25 g (1 oz) fresh coriander in a blender, fry as above and stir into the lentils with 300 ml (½ pint) extra stock. Season and cook, uncovered, for 10 minutes. Allow to cool. Reheat when ready to serve.

# roasted garlic & celeriac soup

Preparation time **25 minutes**
Cooking time **45 minutes**
Finishing time **5 minutes**
Serves **4**

2 small heads of **garlic**, halved
3 teaspoons **olive oil**
25 g (1 oz) **butter**
500 g (1 lb) **celeriac**, peeled
    and cut into chunks
1 **onion**, roughly chopped
1 litre (1¾ pints) **vegetable
    stock**
150 ml (¼ pint) **milk**
40 g (1½ oz) sliced **pancetta**
150 ml (¼ pint) single **cream**
**salt** and **pepper**

**Put** the halved unpeeled garlic heads into a small roasting tin, drizzle with 1 teaspoon of the oil and roast in a preheated oven, 200°C (400°F), Gas Mark 6, for 15 minutes. Meanwhile, heat the remaining oil and the butter in a saucepan, add the celeriac and onion, cover and fry gently for 10 minutes, shaking the pan from time to time.

**Take** the garlic out of its paper skins with the tip of a small knife and add to the celeriac. Pour in the stock, add a little seasoning and bring to the boil. Cover and simmer for 30 minutes, or until the celeriac is tender. Cool slightly.

**Purée** the soup in batches in a food processor or blender then pour back into the pan. Cool completely then chill until required.

**When** ready to serve, stir the milk into the soup and reheat until piping hot. Dry fry the pancetta until crisp and golden and cut into long thin strips. Stir half the cream into the soup then ladle into serving bowls. Swirl the remaining cream into the soup. Sprinkle the soup with the pancetta and serve immediately.

**For roasted garlic & pumpkin soup**, use 500 g (1 lb) deseeded pumpkin. Peel and chop, then use the pumpkin instead of the celeriac. Garnish with cream as above, adding toasted pumpkin seeds instead of pancetta.

# black bean soup with noodles

Preparation time **15 minutes**
Finishing time **10 minutes**
Serves **4**

2 tablespoons groundnut or
  vegetable **oil**
bunch of **spring onions**,
  sliced
2 **garlic** cloves, roughly
  chopped
1 red **chilli**, deseeded and
  sliced
4 cm (1½ inch) piece of fresh
  root **ginger**, peeled and
  grated
125 ml (4 fl oz) **black bean
  sauce**
750 ml (1¼ pints) **vegetable
  stock**
200 g (7 oz) **pak choi** or
  **spring greens**, shredded
2 teaspoons **soy sauce**
1 teaspoon caster **sugar**
50 g (2 oz) raw, unsalted
  shelled **peanuts**
200 g (7 oz) dried soba
  **noodles**, cooked

**Prepare** all the vegetables in advance. When ready to serve, heat the oil in a saucepan. Add the spring onions and garlic and fry gently for 1 minute. Add the chilli, ginger, black bean sauce and stock and bring to the boil.

**Stir** in the pak choi or spring greens, soy sauce, sugar and peanuts, reduce the heat and simmer gently, uncovered, for 4 minutes.

**Pile** the cooked noodles into four serving bowls. Ladle the soup over the noodles and serve immediately.

**For miso broth with prawns & noodles**, fry the spring onions and garlic as above. Add the chilli, ginger and fish stock instead of the vegetable stock, 2 tablespoons miso, 2 tablespoons mirin, soy and sugar as above. Cook for 5 minutes and allow to cool. Finish with 100 g (3½ oz) pak choi, 150 g (5 oz) cooked prawns and 150 g (5 oz) cooked soba noodles.

# tomato soup with tio pepe

Preparation time **25 minutes**
Cooking time **30 minutes**
Finishing time **5 minutes**
Serves **4**

500 g (1 lb) plum **tomatoes**,
    halved
2 tablespoons **olive oil**
1 **onion**, roughly chopped
½ teaspoon **smoked paprika**
50 g (2 oz) **sun-dried**
    **tomatoes** in oil, drained and
    roughly chopped
450 ml (¾ pint) **vegetable**
    **stock**
2–3 tablespoons Tio Pepe dry
    **sherry**
1 teaspoon caster **sugar**
**salt** and **pepper**

**Croûtons**
4 tablespoons **olive oil**
¼ teaspoon **smoked paprika**
125 g (4 oz) rustic white
    **bread**, cubed

**Put** the tomatoes, cut sides up, in the base of a grill pan, drizzle with 1 tablespoon of the oil, season and cook under a preheated hot grill for 5 minutes until browned. Heat the remaining oil in a saucepan, add the onion and fry for 5 minutes until pale golden. Stir in the paprika and cook for 1 minute. Add the grilled tomatoes and crush with a wooden spoon, then mix in the sun-dried tomatoes, stock, sherry and sugar, and season to taste with salt and pepper. Bring to the boil then cover and simmer for 20 minutes.

**Meanwhile**, make the croûtons. Mix the oil and paprika together in a plastic bag, add the cubed bread and toss together. Tip out on to a baking sheet and cook in a preheated oven, 200°C (400°F), Gas Mark 6, for 10 minutes or until crisp and golden.

**Cool** the soup slightly then purée in batches in a blender or food processor until smooth. Sieve and return to the saucepan, cover and set aside until required. When ready to serve, reheat the soup until piping hot, ladle into small bowls and sprinkle with the croûtons and a little olive oil.

### For roasted red pepper soup with Tio Pepe,

omit the tomatoes. Fry 1 chopped onion and mix in ½ teaspoon paprika as above. Drain and chop the peppers from a 680 g (1½ lb) jar of roasted peppers and mix with 50 g (2 oz) sun-dried tomatoes. Finish as above.

# broccoli & cheddar soup

Preparation time **10 minutes**
Cooking time **30 minutes**
Finishing time **5 minutes**
Serves **6**

1 kg (2 lb) **broccoli**
50 g (2 oz) **butter**
1 **onion**, chopped
1 large **potato**, peeled and
quartered
1.5 litres (2½ pints) **vegetable
stock**
125 ml (4 fl oz) single **cream**
1 tablespoon **lemon juice**
1 teaspoon **Worcestershire
sauce**
a few drops of **Tabasco
sauce**
125 g (4 oz) mature **Cheddar**
cheese, grated
**salt** and **pepper**

**Remove** all the tough stems and leaves from the broccoli. Cut off the stalks, peel them and cut them into 2.5 cm (1 inch) pieces. Break the florets into very small pieces and set them aside.

**Melt** the butter in a large saucepan. Add the onion and broccoli stalks and cook, covered, for 5 minutes over a medium heat, stirring frequently.

**Add** the broccoli florets, potato and vegetable stock to the pan. Bring the mixture to the boil and cook, partially covered, for 5 minutes. Using a slotted spoon, remove 6 or more florets for a garnish and set aside. Season the mixture with salt and pepper and continue to cook for 20 minutes, or until all the vegetables are soft.

**Using** a blender or food processor, purée the mixture in batches until smooth, transferring each successive batch to a clean saucepan. Chill until required.

**When** ready to serve, add the cream, lemon juice, Worcestershire sauce and a few drops of Tabasco to the pan. Heat the soup gently and simmer for 3–5 minutes, but do not allow the soup to boil. Just before serving, stir in the grated cheese. Serve the soup, garnished with the reserved broccoli or watercress, if liked.

**For creamy cauliflower & Cheddar soup**, cut 1 large cauliflower into small florets. Fry in 25 g (1 oz) butter and 1 tablespoon olive oil with 1 chopped onion as above. Add 600 ml (1 pint) vegetable stock, season and simmer for 10 minutes. Purée in batches, return to the pan. Chill until required. Stir in 450 ml (¾ pint) milk, 2 teaspoons Dijon mustard and a little grated nutmeg. Reheat and stir in 75 g (3 oz) grated Cheddar.

# fish mousse with walnut salad

Preparation time **20 minutes**
Cooking time **3–4 minutes**
Finishing time **5 minutes**
Serves **4**

150 g (5 oz) sliced **cold-
smoked rainbow trout** or
**smoked salmon**
100 g (3½ oz) full-fat **crème
fraîche**
finely grated rind of ½ **lemon**
1 tablespoon **lemon juice**
175 g (6 oz) mixed **hot-
smoked fish** (trout, salmon
and mackerel fillet)
**salt** and **pepper**

**Salad**
25 g (1 oz) **walnut pieces**
3 tablespoons **olive oil**
1 tablespoon red wine
**vinegar**
40 g (1½ oz) **watercress**

**Line** 4 150 ml (¼ pint) pudding moulds or china
ramekin dishes with clingfilm, then line the bases and
sides with the sliced trout, keeping a little back for
putting on the tops.

**Mix** the crème fraîche, lemon rind and lemon juice with
a little black pepper. Flake the fish, discarding any skin
and bones, then fold it into the crème fraîche mixture.
Divide between the lined moulds then cover with the
remaining sliced trout. Fold any overhanging pieces of
trout over the top then chill until required.

**To** make the salad dressing, toast the walnuts in a dry
frying pan over a medium heat until lightly browned.
Mix the oil, vinegar and a little seasoning together then
add to the hot walnuts and set aside.

**When** ready to serve, tear any very long stems off the
watercress then toss with the dressing. Unmould the
mousses, remove the clingfilm and arrange on 4 small
plates. Spoon the salad around and serve with warmed
crusty brown rolls, if liked.

**For smoked fish toasts with walnut salad**, omit the
cold smoked rainbow trout. Make the crème fraîche,
lemon and hot smoked fish mix as above. Spread onto
toasted slices of thin wholewheat baguette. Serve
with salad leaves tossed in lemon juice as above.

# grilled aubergine parcels

Preparation time **15 minutes**
Cooking time **2 minutes**
Finishing time **10 minutes**
Serves **4**

1 long, large **aubergine**
125 g (4 oz) **mozzarella**
  cheese
1 large or 2 small plum
  **tomatoes**
8 large **basil** leaves
1 tablespoon **olive oil**
1 tablespoon **pine nuts**,
  dry-fried in a hot pan
  until golden
**salt** and **pepper**

**Tomato dressing**
2 tablespoons **olive oil**
1 teaspoon balsamic **vinegar**
1 teaspoon **sun-dried tomato
  paste**
1 teaspoon **lemon juice**

**Remove** the stalk from the aubergine and cut it lengthwise into 8 slices, disregarding the 2 outer edges. Put the aubergine slices in a pan of boiling salted water and cook for 2 minutes, then drain and dry on kitchen paper. Cut the mozzarella into 4 slices and the tomato into 8 slices, disregarding the outer edges.

**Place** 2 of the aubergine slices in a flameproof dish, forming a cross. Place a slice of tomato on top, season with salt and pepper, add a basil leaf, a slice of mozzarella, another basil leaf, then more salt and pepper, and finally another slice of tomato. Fold the edges of the aubergine around the filling. Repeat with the other ingredients to make 4 parcels in total. Cover and chill for 20 minutes, or until required.

**To** make the dressing, whisk together the oil, vinegar, tomato paste and lemon juice. Cover and set aside until required.

**When** ready to serve, brush the aubergine parcels with olive oil. Place the dish under a preheated hot grill and cook for about 5 minutes on each side, until golden brown. Serve hot, drizzled with the dressing and scattered with the pine nuts and extra basil leaves.

**For aubergine & tomato salad**, drain a 200 g (7 oz) chilled carton roasted aubergine and red peppers, reserving the oil. Arrange in a dish with 4 sliced plum tomatoes, 250 g (8 oz) drained, sliced mozzarella, a small bunch of torn basil leaves and a few black olives. Make the dressing by mixing 3 tablespoons of the reserved oil, 1 tablespoon red wine vinegar and 1 finely chopped garlic clove and season.

# potted crab & prawns

Preparation time **20 minutes**, plus chilling
Cooking time **10 minutes**
Finishing time **5 minutes**
Serves **4**

200 g (7 oz) **butter**, diced
finely grated rind and juice of
  1 **lime**
3 tablespoons chopped
  **coriander**
generous pinch of **cayenne
  pepper**
200 g (7 oz) peeled, cooked
  **prawns**, roughly chopped
1 dressed **crab**, about 175 g
  (6 oz)
½ small wholemeal **baguette**,
  sliced
2 heads of **chicory**
a few tiny **radishes**
**salt**

**First** clarify the butter. Heat a small saucepan of water, add the butter and heat gently until melted. Cool, then freeze until the butter has formed a set layer on top of the water. Lift the disc of hardened butter off the water and discard the water. Remove any droplets of water from the underside of the butter with kitchen paper.

**Melt** half the clarified butter in a saucepan. Add the lime rind, chopped coriander, cayenne and a little salt. Stir the prawns into the butter with the crab meat and lime juice. Heat until piping hot. Spoon into 4 small china ramekins and press down well so there are no air pockets. Chill for 15 minutes.

**Melt** the remaining butter in a clean pan then spoon over the top of the fish mixture in a thin even layer. Chill for 3–4 hours until set. Sprinkle with a little extra cayenne.

**When** ready to serve, toast the bread then arrange on plates with the dishes of potted fish. Serve with chicory leaves and tiny radishes.

**For potted prawns with chives**, use chopped chives instead of the coriander. Replace the lime rind and juice with the finely grated rind of 1 lemon and 2 tablespoons lemon juice. Use 375 g (12 oz) prawns in place of the crab and prawns.

# chicken satay

Preparation time **10 minutes**,
plus marinating
Finishing time **10 minutes**
Serves **6**

25 g (1 oz) smooth **peanut
butter**
125 ml (4 fl oz) **soy sauce**
125 ml (4 fl oz) **lime juice**
15 g (½ oz) **curry powder**
2 **garlic** cloves, chopped
1 teaspoon **hot pepper sauce**
6 skinless **chicken** breast
fillets, cubed

**Combine** the peanut butter, soy sauce, lime juice, curry powder, garlic and hot pepper sauce in a non-metallic dish. Add the chicken, mix well and chill for 12 hours or until required.

**When** ready to serve, divide the chicken cubes between 6 metal skewers and cook under a preheated hot grill for 5 minutes on each side until tender and cooked through. Serve immediately with lemon wedges and chunks of cucumber and onion, if liked.

**For miso-grilled chicken**, mix 2 tablespoons each soy sauce, dry sherry or rice wine, and 2 teaspoons clear honey and miso paste. Add the cubed chicken and marinate as above. Thread on to skewers and cook as above. Serve with rice and a sliced cucumber and red chilli salad.

# black olive tapenade toasts

Preparation time **15 minutes**
Cooking time **3–4 minutes**
Finishing time **10 minutes**
Serves **4**

12 slices of thin **baguette**
1 **garlic** clove, halved
200 g (7 oz) marinated, pitted
  mixed **olives**
2 tablespoons **olive oil**
small bunch of **basil**
25 g (1 oz) **pecorino** or
  **Parmesan** cheese, grated

**Toast** the bread lightly on both sides then rub one side with the garlic. Transfer to a baking sheet.

**Finely** chop the olives in a blender or food processor, then add the oil and most of the basil and blend again to make a coarse paste. Spread over the garlic toasts. Cover loosely and chill until required.

**When** ready to serve, remove the cover and cook the toasts in a preheated oven, 190°C (375°F), Gas Mark 5, for 10 minutes. Arrange on a serving plate and sprinkle with the pecorino or Parmesan and the remaining basil leaves.

**For broad bean tapenade toasts**, fry ½ chopped onion and 1 finely chopped garlic clove in 1 tablespoon olive oil for 5 minutes until softened. Add 200 g (7 oz) frozen broad beans and 75 ml (3 fl oz) vegetable stock, then simmer for 5 minutes. Mash or process until a coarse paste, stir in 2 tablespoons lemon juice, a small bunch of chopped parsley or coriander and salt and pepper. When ready to serve, toast 4 pitta breads, tear into strips and top with bean paste. Garnish with extra herbs.

# fresh broad bean & chilli dip

Preparation time **5 minutes**
Cooking time **10 minutes**
Finishing time **5 minutes**
Serves **4**

375 g (12 oz) fresh or frozen
  **broad beans**
50 g (2 oz) **parsley**, coarsely
  chopped
50 g (2 oz) **coriander**,
  coarsely chopped
1–2 mild green **chillies**,
  deseeded and chopped
2 **garlic** cloves, chopped
1½ teaspoons ground **cumin**
3 tablespoons **olive oil**
1 **onion**, thinly sliced
**salt**

**Cook** the beans in a pan of boiling salted water for 5 minutes. Add the herbs, cover and simmer for a further 5 minutes. Drain, reserving some of the cooking liquid.

**Place** the cooked beans in a blender or food processor with the chillies, garlic, cumin, 2 tablespoons of the oil and 3–4 tablespoons of the reserved cooking liquid. Process to a smooth paste, season to taste and add a little more cooking liquid if it is too dry. Transfer to a serving dish and chill until required.

**When** ready to serve, heat the remaining oil in a non-stick frying pan and fry the onion briskly until golden and crisp. Spread over the dip and serve with crudités or wholemeal pitta breads.

**For avocado & chilli dip**, drain 410 g (13½ oz) can chickpeas and put in a blender with 2 tablespoons toasted sesame seeds, 1 mild deseeded red chilli, 4 tablespoons lemon juice, 2 finely chopped garlic cloves, 100 g (3½ oz) natural yogurt and seasoning. Blend until smooth then set aside. When ready to serve, add the flesh of 1 avocado and blend again. Serve with warm pitta breads.

# mini bacon, prune & stilton grills

Preparation time **15 minutes**
Finishing time **10–15 minutes**
Serves **4**

75 g (3 oz) **Stilton** cheese,
  rind removed
16 large pitted ready-to-eat
  **prunes**
8 rashers of streaky **bacon**
20 g (¾ oz) **butter**
4 slices of **bread**

**Cut** the cheese into 16 squares, make a slit in each prune then insert a cube of cheese. Cut each rasher of bacon in half and wrap one half around each stuffed prune.

**Lightly** butter the slices of bread, cut each into 4 squares and arrange on a baking sheet. Place one prune on the top of each piece of bread, then secure in place with a cocktail stick. Cover and chill until required.

**When** ready to serve, remove the cover and bake in a preheated oven, 200°C (400°F), Gas Mark 6, for 10–15 minutes until the bread and bacon are crisp and golden and the cheese just melted. Arrange on one large serving plate or individual plates, garnished with rocket.

**For angels on horseback**, wrap 16 shelled oysters in halved bacon rashers and hold in place with cocktail sticks. Grill the bacon-wrapped oysters and squares of buttered bread separately until just cooked, then assemble and serve immediately.

# nut koftas with minted yogurt

Preparation time **15 minutes**
Cooking time **5 minutes**
Finishing time **10 minutes**
Serves **4**

6 tablespoons vegetable **oil**
1 **onion**, chopped
½ teaspoon crushed **chilli
flakes**
2 **garlic** cloves, roughly
chopped
1 tablespoon medium **curry
paste**
425 g (14 oz) can **borlotti** or
**cannellini beans**, rinsed and
drained
125 g (4 oz) ground **almonds**
75 g (3 oz) salted **almonds**,
chopped
1 small **egg**
200 ml (7 fl oz) Greek **yogurt**
2 tablespoons chopped **mint**
1 tablespoon **lemon juice**
8 mini **naan breads**
**salt** and **pepper**

**Heat** 3 tablespoons of the oil in a frying pan, add the
onion and fry for 4 minutes. Add the chilli flakes, garlic
and curry paste and fry for 1 minute.

**Transfer** to a food processor or blender with the
beans, ground almonds, salted almonds, egg and a
little salt and pepper and process until the mixture
starts to bind together.

**Using** lightly floured hands, take about one-eighth
of the mixture and mould it around a metal skewer,
forming it into a sausage about 2.5 cm (1 inch) thick.
Make 7 more koftas in the same way. Cover and chill
until required.

**Mix** together the yogurt and mint in a small serving
bowl and season to taste with salt and pepper. In a
separate bowl, mix together 2 tablespoons oil, lemon
juice and a little salt and pepper. Cover both bowls
and chill until required.

**When** ready to serve, place the koftas on a foil-lined
grill rack and brush with 1 tablespoon of oil. Cook
under a preheated moderate grill for about 5 minutes
until golden, turning once. Brush the koftas with the
lemon dressing and serve in warm naan breads,
drizzled with the yogurt dressing.

**For spiced lamb koftas**, mix 500 g (1 lb) minced
lamb with 4 finely chopped spring onions and
1 teaspoon each ground cumin and ground coriander.
Season well, shape into small balls and chill until
required. Thread on to metal skewers and grill for
about 10 minutes, turning until cooked through.
Serve with yogurt and naan breads as above.

# marinated prawn skewers

Preparation time **20 minutes**
Finishing time **7–8 minutes**
Serves **4**

400 g (13 oz) raw **tiger
    prawns** in their shells
finely grated rind and juice of
    1 **lemon**
finely grated rind and juice of
    1 **lime**
1 tablespoon sesame **oil**
2 **garlic** cloves, finely chopped
**salt** and **pepper**

**Pickled cucumber salad**
½ **cucumber**
¼–½ mild red **chilli**, deseeded
    and finely chopped
2 tablespoons chopped
    **coriander**
1 tablespoon white wine
    **vinegar**
1 teaspoon **Thai fish sauce**
½ teaspoon caster **sugar**
fresh **coriander** and **lime**
    wedges to garnish, optional

**Divide** the prawns between 8 wooden skewers. In a shallow ceramic dish long enough to hold the skewers, beat together the grated rind and juice of the lemon and lime, the oil and garlic. Season with salt and pepper, add the prawn skewers and coat in the marinade. Cover and chill until required.

**Very** thinly slice the cucumber and put into a shallow dish. Sprinkle with the chilli, coriander, vinegar, fish sauce and sugar. Cover and chill until required.

**When** ready to serve, place the skewers under a preheated hot grill with the exposed parts of the skewers away from the heat. Cook for 7–8 minutes, turning once, until the prawns are bright pink all over. Stir the salad and spoon in to small bowls set on plates. Add two skewers to each plate, and garnish with coriander sprigs and lime wedges, if liked.

**For marinated beef skewers**, cut 625 g (1¼ lb) sirloin steak into cubes, then thread on to skewers and marinate in 3 tablespoons good-quality bought teriyaki marinade and the grated rind and juice of 1 lime. Grill as above and serve with a pickled cucumber salad.

# aubergine pâté

Preparation time **10 minutes**, plus soaking

Cooking time **15 minutes**

Serves **6**

25 g (1 oz) dried **porcini mushrooms**
6 tablespoons **olive oil**
500 g (1 lb) **aubergines**, cut into 1 cm (½ inch) dice
1 small red **onion**, chopped
2 teaspoons **cumin** seeds
175 g (6 oz) **chestnut mushrooms**
2 **garlic** cloves, crushed
3 **pickled walnuts**, halved
small handful of **coriander**
**salt** and **pepper**

**Place** the dried mushrooms in a bowl and cover with boiling water. Leave to soak for 10 minutes.

**Meanwhile**, heat the oil in a large frying pan. Add the aubergines and onion and fry gently for 8 minutes until the vegetables are softened and browned.

**Drain** the dried mushrooms and add to the pan with the cumin seeds, fresh mushrooms and garlic. Fry for a further 5–7 minutes until the aubergines are very soft.

**Transfer** the mixture to a food processor or blender with the pickled walnuts and coriander, season to taste with salt and pepper and process until broken up but not completely smooth. Transfer to a serving dish and chill until required. Serve the pâté on thick slices of bread or hot toast.

**For mushroom chakchouka**, make as above, adding the mushroom soaking liquid and 400 g (13 oz) canned chopped tomatoes to the pan with the dried and fresh mushrooms. Cover and simmer for 15 minutes, then allow to cool. Reheat when needed. Serve with warm pitta breads, and top each portion with a poached egg and some fresh coriander.

# red pepper & munster tartlets

Preparation time **15 minutes**,
plus chilling
Cooking time **15 minutes**
Finishing time **25–30 minutes**
Serves **4**

400 g (13 oz) ready-made
  **shortcrust pastry**
1 tablespoon vegetable **oil**
15 g (½ oz) **butter**
1 red **onion**, finely chopped
150 ml (¼ pint) single **cream**
2 **eggs**
2 **garlic** cloves, crushed
15 g (½ oz) **chives**, snipped
1 small **red pepper**, roasted,
  peeled and thinly sliced
75 g (3 oz) **Munster** cheese,
  roughly chopped
**salt** and **pepper**

**Roll** out the pastry on a lightly floured surface and use to line four 10 cm (4 inch) tartlet tins. Prick the bases, line with circles of greaseproof paper and fill with baking beans, then chill for 30 minutes.

**Place** the tartlets on a baking sheet and bake blind in a preheated oven, 190°C (375°F), Gas Mark 5, for 8 minutes. Remove the paper and beans and bake for a further 2–3 minutes, or until the shells are crisp and beginning to brown. Remove from the oven and set aside until required.

**Heat** the oil and butter in a pan and fry the red onion until caramelized. Set aside until required. Beat the cream, eggs, salt and pepper together. Add the crushed garlic and chives, and chill the mixture until required.

**When** ready to serve, divide the onion and the roasted red pepper strips between the pastry shells. Pour over the cream and egg mixture and sprinkle the Munster on top. Cook the tartlets on the middle shelf of a preheated oven, 190°C (375°F), Gas Mark 5, for 20–25 minutes, or until just cooked. Garnish with basil leaves and snipped chives, if liked.

**For leek & Gruyère tarts**, make the pastry cases as above. Fry 2 small thinly sliced leeks in oil and butter then divide them equally between the tart cases. Add the cream mixture as above and 75 g (3 oz) grated Gruyère instead of the munster.

# aïoli with vegetable dippers

Preparation time **15 minutes**
Finishing time **3 minutes**
Serves **4**

3 **garlic** cloves
2 **egg yolks**
1 teaspoon Dijon **mustard**
250 ml (8 fl oz) **olive oil**
2 tablespoons **lemon juice**
**salt** and **pepper**

**Dippers**
125 g (4 oz) baby **carrots**,
   scrubbed, halved
125 g (4 oz) **asparagus tips**
75 g (3 oz) **sugar snap peas**
1 **little gem lettuce**, leaves
   separated

**Crush** the garlic in a pestle and mortar with a little salt and pepper. Transfer to a large mixing bowl and add the egg yolks and mustard.

**Whisk** the ingredients together with a balloon whisk or electric whisk until just mixed, then gradually trickle in the oil, drop by drop to begin with, until the mixture begins to thicken. Then continue with the oil in a very thin steady stream until about half has been added.

**Thin** the mayonnaise with a little lemon juice, then continue whisking in the oil very gradually until very thick. Taste and add a little more lemon juice if you like. Cover and chill until required.

**Blanche** the asparagus and sugar snaps in a saucepan of boiling water for 2 minutes. Drain and allow to cool. Put all of the vegetables into a plastic bag and chill with the aïoli until required.

**When** ready to serve, spoon the aïoli into a bowl and set on to a large platter. Arrange the vegetables around the bowl and serve.

Note: If the aïoli should 'split' or separate while you are making it, don't panic. Put 1 egg yolk into a separate bowl and then very gradually whisk the split mixture into the new egg yolk until smooth once more.

**For green mayonnaise with dippers**, omit the garlic and stir 50 g (2 oz) very finely chopped watercress into the mayonnaise at the end. Serve with strips of pepper, breadsticks or blanched asparagus.

# caramelized brie

Preparation time **10 minutes**
Finishing time **20 minutes**,
plus standing
Serves **4**

400 g (13 oz) ready-made
  **puff pastry**
1 small **egg**
1 tablespoon **milk**
pinch of **salt**
2 small wheels of **Brie** cheese

**Divide** the pastry into 4 and roll out each piece on a lightly floured surface to form a thin round, 5 cm (2 inches) larger than the cheeses.

**Make** an egg glaze by beating together the egg, milk and salt in a small bowl. Place each cheese wheel in the middle of a pastry round. Brush the pastry around the cheese with a little of the egg glaze and then top each with a second pastry round. Press all around the edges of the pastry rounds to seal the pieces together well, then trim the excess pastry to give a 2.5 cm (1 inch) border.

**Transfer** the cheeses to a baking sheet. Brush the tops and sides with more of the egg glaze and score the tops with a sharp knife to form a pattern. Cut 2 small slits in each top to allow steam to escape. Chill until required.

**When** ready to serve, bake the cheeses in a preheated oven, 220°C (425°F), Gas Mark 7, for 20 minutes until the pastry is puffed up and golden. Allow to stand for 10 minutes before garnishing with parsley and shredded beetroot.

**For baked Brie with cranberries**, unwrap the cheeses, line the boxes with non-stick baking paper and replace the cheeses. Top each cheese with 1 tablespoon cranberry sauce and ¼ chopped red onion. When ready to serve, bake uncovered at 180°C (350°F), Gas Mark 4, for 5–10 minutes until warmed and soft. Serve with apple slices, cucumber, celery and breadstick dippers.

# tortillas with aubergine yogurt

Preparation time **10 minutes**
Cooking time **10 minutes**
Serves **4**

4 tablespoons **olive oil**
1 **aubergine**, thinly sliced
small handful of **mint**,
   chopped
small handful of chopped
   **parsley**
2 tablespoons chopped
   **chives**
1 green **chilli**, deseeded and
   thinly sliced
200 ml (7 fl oz) Greek **yogurt**
2 tablespoons **mayonnaise**
2 large **tortillas**
7 cm (3 inch) length of
   **cucumber**, thinly sliced
**salt**, **pepper** and **paprika**

**Heat** the oil in a frying pan. Add the aubergine and fry for about 10 minutes until golden on both sides. Drain and set aside to cool.

**Mix** the herbs with the chilli, yogurt and mayonnaise in a bowl and season to taste with salt and pepper.

**Arrange** the fried aubergine slices over the tortillas and spread with the Greek yogurt mixture. Arrange the cucumber slices on top. Roll up each tortilla, sprinkle with paprika and cut into thick slices. Chill until required.

**For mexican turkey tortillas**, fry 300 g (10 oz) minced turkey in 1 tablespoon sunflower oil for 10 minutes until lightly browned. Stir in 1 teaspoon roughly crushed cumin seeds, 1 teaspoon paprika and ½ teaspoon chilli powder. Cook for 5 minutes, then cover and chill. When ready to serve, reheat the mince and divide between 8 warmed tortillas. Top with 200 g (7 oz) natural yogurt, ½ small shredded iceberg lettuce, 2 diced tomatoes and some torn coriander leaves. Roll up tightly and serve immediately.

# salads &
# light lunches

# lentil, chorizo & scallop salad

Preparation time **10 minutes**
Cooking time **15–20 minutes**
Finishing time **5–6 minutes**
Serves **4**

250 g (8 oz) puy **lentils**
2 **red peppers**, quartered,
  cored and deseeded
6 tablespoons **olive oil**
3 tablespoons balsamic
  **vinegar**
150 g (5 oz) **chorizo**, thinly
  sliced or diced
375 g (12 oz) **scallops**, rinsed
  and patted dry
75 g (3 oz) **rocket** leaves
**salt** and **pepper**

**Cook** the lentils in a saucepan of simmering water for 15–20 minutes until just tender but still holding their shape. Drain the lentils, rinse in cold water and drain again.

**Meanwhile**, arrange the peppers, cut sides down, on a piece of foil on a grill rack, brush with 1 tablespoon of the oil and grill for 10–15 minutes until softened and lightly charred. Wrap in foil while hot. When cool enough to handle, remove the skins and slice the flesh.

**Mix** 4 tablespoons of the oil in a bowl with the vinegar and a little seasoning. Add the lentils and toss well, then stir in the pepper strips. Cover and set aside.

**When** ready to serve, heat the remaining 1 tablespoon of oil in a frying pan, add the chorizo and fry for 2 minutes. Add the scallops and cook for 3–4 minutes, turning once, until browned and just cooked. Divide the rocket leaves between 4 serving plates. Spoon the lentils on top, then add the chorizo and scallops and serve immediately.

**For warm goats' cheese & lentil salad**, cook the lentils and peppers as above. Slice 175 g (6 oz) goats' cheese and arrange on the oiled foil on the grill rack. Sprinkle with pepper, some torn rosemary leaves and a drizzle of olive oil. Grill until just beginning to melt, then transfer to the top of the lentil salad.

# hot haloumi with fattoush salad

Preparation time **10 minutes**
Finishing time **5 minutes**
Serves **4**

40 g (1½ oz) finely sliced **red pepper**
40 g (1½ oz) finely sliced **yellow pepper**
40 g (1½ oz) chopped **cucumber**
40 g (1½ oz) finely chopped **spring onions**
1 tablespoon chopped **parsley**
1 tablespoon chopped **mint**
1 tablespoon chopped **coriander**
2 teaspoons **olive oil**
125 g (4 oz) **haloumi** cheese, thickly sliced

**Dressing**
½ teaspoon crushed **garlic**
1 tablespoon **olive oil**
2 tablespoons **lemon juice**
**salt** and **pepper**

**Put** the red and yellow peppers, cucumber, spring onions, parsley, mint and coriander in a bowl. Mix well, cover and chill until required.

**To** make the dressing, mix the garlic with the oil and lemon juice and season with salt and pepper to taste. Set aside until required.

**When** ready to serve, pour the dressing over the salad and toss lightly to mix. Transfer to a serving plate. Heat the oil in a frying pan and fry the haloumi over a medium to high heat for 1–2 minutes on each side until golden brown. Arrange the haloumi on top of the salad and serve immediately.

**For lemon-dressed haloumi & grape salad**, mix 3 tablespoons olive oil with 2 tablespoons lemon juice and 1 teaspoon honey, then season well. Mix 125 g (4 oz) halved green and black seedless grapes with 125 g (4 oz) mixed salad leaves and 2 tablespoons fresh coriander. Chill the leaves and dressing separately. When ready to serve, fry the haloumi as above, toss the dressing with the salad, spoon on to plates and top with the cheese.

# picnic pie

Preparation time **35 minutes**
Cooking time **1½ hours**
Serves **6–8**

175 g (6 oz) **lard**
175 ml (6 fl oz) **milk** and
 **water** mixed
2 teaspoons English **mustard**
375 g (12 oz) plain **flour**
½ teaspoon **salt**

**Filling**
500 g (1 lb) lean pork and leek
 or Cumberland **sausages**,
 skinned
500 g (1 lb) skinless boneless
 **chicken** thighs, chopped
125 g (4 oz) smoked **bacon**,
 diced
5 **cloves**, roughly crushed
¼ teaspoon ground **allspice**
small bunch of **sage**
1 Braeburn **apple**, cored
 and sliced
1 **egg yolk** mixed with
 1 tablespoon **water**
**salt** and **pepper**

**First** make the pastry. Heat the lard in the milk and water in a small saucepan until melted then stir in the mustard. Mix the flour and salt in a bowl then stir in the melted lard mixture and mix to a soft ball. Cool for 10 minutes. Mix the sausagemeat, chicken, bacon, cloves, allspice and plenty of seasoning together in a bowl.

**Remove** one-third of the pastry and set aside. Press the remaining warm pastry over the base and sides of a deep 18 cm (7 inch) loose-bottomed cake tin. Spoon in half the filling and level. Cover with half the sage leaves, then the apple slices, then spoon over the rest of the filling. Level and top with the remaining sage. Brush the edges of the pastry with the egg glaze.

**Roll** the reserved pastry to a circle a little larger than the tin, arrange on the pie and press the edges together. Trim off the excess then crimp the edge. Make a slit in the top of the pie, then brush with egg glaze. Cook in a preheated oven, 180°C (350°F), Gas Mark 4, for 1½ hours, covering with foil after 40 minutes, when golden. Leave to cool, remove the tin then put the pie, still on the tin base, in the refrigerator for 3–4 hours or overnight. When ready to serve, remove the base and cut the pie into wedges.

**For apricot & pickled onion pie**, make up the filling as above, but omit the sage and apples, instead adding 100 g (3½ oz) sliced ready-to-eat dried apricots and 100 g (3½ oz) drained and sliced pickled onions.

# wasabi & ginger tofu salad

Preparation time **15 minutes**
Finishing time **5 minutes**
Serves **4**

100 g (3½ oz) firm **tofu**, sliced
　　into thin strips
½ teaspoon **olive oil**

**Marinade**
1 teaspoon **olive oil**
1 tablespoon **soy sauce**
1 **garlic** clove, crushed
2.5 cm (1 inch) piece of fresh
　　root **ginger**, peeled and
　　finely grated
1 teaspoon **lemon juice**
½ teaspoon **wasabi paste**

**Alfalfa salad**
75 g (3 oz) shredded **lettuce**
1 small **tomato**, sliced
2 teaspoons finely chopped
　　**spring onion**
1 **garlic** clove, crushed
½ **fennel** bulb, finely sliced
25 g (1 oz) **alfalfa sprouts**
25 g (1 oz) **sunflower seeds**
1 tablespoon **lime juice**
½ **avocado**, sliced
**salt** and **pepper**
1 tablespoon **olive oil**

**To** make the marinade, mix the olive oil, soy sauce, garlic, ginger, lemon juice and wasabi in a shallow, non-metallic dish. Add the tofu, stir well and chill until required.

**To** make the salad, put the lettuce, tomato, spring onion, garlic, avocado, fennel and alfalfa sprouts in a bowl. Add the sunflower seeds and lime juice. Season with salt and pepper and toss well. Cover and chill until required.

**When** ready to serve, heat a heavy-based frying pan and add a small amount of oil. Fry the tofu strips until golden brown on both sides. Peel, stone and slice the avocado and add to the salad with the oil. Toss and top with tofu. Serve immediately with the alfalfa salad.

**For sizzling tofu with gingered greens**, arrange 250 g (8 oz) sliced tofu on a foil-lined grill rack and brush with a mixture of 2 teaspoons sesame oil and 2 tablespoons soy sauce. Stand 15 minutes, then grill for 4–5 minutes, turning once. Stir-fry 500 g (1 lb) sliced pak choi with 2 teaspoons sunflower oil, 2 teaspoons sesame oil, 2 chopped garlic cloves, 2 sliced shallots and 2 tablespoons finely chopped fresh root ginger. Add 1 tablespoon soy sauce, mix well and serve with the tofu.

# salmon & new potato salad

Preparation time **20 minutes**
Cooking time **12–14 minutes**
Finishing time **2 minutes**
Serves **4**

750 g (1½ lb) baby new
**potatoes**, thickly sliced
4 **salmon** steaks, about 125 g
(4 oz) each
6 tablespoons **olive oil**
finely grated rind and juice of
1 **lemon**
2 teaspoons runny **honey**
1 red **onion**, halved and thinly
sliced
1 tablespoon **capers**, roughly
chopped, and 2 teaspoons
brine from the jar
50 g (2 oz) can **anchovies** in
oil, drained and roughly
chopped
small bunch of **parsley**,
roughly torn
**salt** and **pepper**

**Half-fill** the base of a steamer with water, bring
to the boil then add the potatoes to the water.
Season the salmon and arrange in a single layer
in the top of the steamer. Cover and cook the
potatoes for 12–14 minutes until just tender, and
the salmon for 8–10 minutes until cooked through.

**Make** the dressing by forking the oil, lemon rind and
juice, honey and seasoning together in the base of
a salad bowl. Add the onion, capers, brine and the
anchovies. Drain the potatoes and toss with the
dressing while still hot. Skin and flake the salmon,
discarding any bones, and arrange on top of the
potatoes. Leave to cool, cover and chill until required.

**When** ready to serve, tear the parsley over the fish and
gently toss the salad together. Serve in shallow bowls.

**For new potato salad with horseradish & bresaola**,
cook the potatoes as above until tender. Make a
dressing by mixing 150 g (5 oz) Greek yogurt with
1 teaspoon grated horseradish (from a jar) and
4 finely chopped spring onions. Add the drained and
cooked potatoes and set aside until ready to serve.
Stir, spoon on to plates and top with 125 g (4 oz)
thinly sliced bresaola.

# panzanella

Preparation time **15 minutes**
Cooking time **10–15 minutes**
Serves **4**

3 **red peppers**, cored,
   deseeded and quartered
375 g (12 oz) ripe plum
   **tomatoes**, skinned
6 tablespoons extra virgin
   **olive oil**
3 tablespoons white wine
   **vinegar**
2 **garlic** cloves, crushed
125 g (4 oz) stale **ciabatta**
   bread, broken into small
   chunks
50 g (2 oz) pitted black **olives**
small handful of **basil** leaves,
   shredded
**salt** and **pepper**

**Place** the peppers, skin side up, on a foil-lined grill
rack and grill under a preheated moderate grill for
10–15 minutes or until the skins are blackened.

**Meanwhile**, quarter the tomatoes and scoop out
the pulp, placing it in a sieve over a bowl to catch
the juices. Set the tomato quarters aside. Press the
pulp with the back of a spoon to extract as much
juice as possible. Beat the oil, vinegar, garlic and
salt and pepper into the tomato juice.

**When** cool enough to handle, peel the skins from
the peppers and discard. Roughly slice the peppers
and place in a bowl with the tomato quarters, bread,
olives and basil. Add the dressing and toss the
ingredients together. Chill until required.

**For baked panzanella**, halve and deseed 2 red
peppers, leaving the stalks intact. Put into a roasting
tin and stuff with 2 skinned and quartered tomatoes,
½ small sliced red onion, 2 chopped garlic cloves and
4 sliced canned anchovy fillets, if liked. Tear 2 slices
ciabatta into coarse crumbs and scatter over the top.
Sprinkle with black pepper and 3 tablespoons olive
oil, then roast at 180°C (350°F), Gas Mark 4, for
45 minutes until tender. Sprinkle with a handful of
basil leaves and serve hot or cold.

# marinated thai beef salad

Preparation time **25 minutes**
Cooking time **15–18 minutes**
Finishing time **5 minutes**
Serves **4**

150 g (5 oz) long-grain white
and wild **rice** mixed
finely grated rind and juice of
2 **limes**
700 g (1 lb 6 oz) thick cut
sirloin or rump **steak**
2 tablespoons sesame **oil**
2 **courgettes**
2 **carrots**
4 **spring onions**, thinly sliced
2 **garlic** cloves, roughly
chopped
1 large mild red **chilli**,
deseeded and chopped
4 cm (1½ inch) piece of fresh
root **ginger**, peeled and cut
into thin strips
2 tablespoons **soy sauce**
4 tablespoons dry **sherry** or
**water**
1 tablespoon **Thai fish sauce**
2 teaspoons caster **sugar**
small bunch of **coriander** or
**mint**, roughly torn

**Cook** the rice in a saucepan of boiling water for
15–18 minutes or until just tender. Drain, rinse in
cold water, drain thoroughly and put into a bowl with
the lime rind and juice and toss together. Cover and
set aside. Brush the steaks with the sesame oil then
cook in a preheated frying pan over a high heat for
1–3 minutes each side, depending on preference.
Transfer to a shallow non-metallic dish.

**Cut** the courgettes and carrots into long thin slices
with a vegetable peeler, add to the hot frying pan with
the spring onion, garlic, chilli and ginger and fry briefly
for 30 seconds. Transfer to the dish with the steak.
Add the soy sauce, sherry or water, fish sauce and
sugar to the pan and warm gently. Pour over the steak
and vegetables, allow to cool, then chill until required.

**When** ready to serve, transfer the rice to a salad bowl.
Add the vegetables and sauce and the torn herbs and
toss to combine. Cut the steak into thin slices and
arrange on top of the rice salad.

**For peppered beef with blue-cheese salad**, brush
2 steaks with olive oil then press them on to a mixture
of crushed peppercorns and sea salt flakes to coat.
Pan-fry as above, then wrap in foil and cool. Make a
dressing by mixing 200 g (7 oz) natural yogurt with
100 g (3½ oz) mashed Stilton and 1 finely chopped
garlic clove. When ready to serve, toss 150 g (5 oz)
mixed salad leaves with 1 thinly sliced red onion and
100 g (3½ oz) sliced button mushrooms with the
dressing. Spoon on to serving plates. Thinly slice the
beef and arrange on top.

# mediterranean rice salad

Preparation time **10 minutes**
Cooking time **5 minutes**
Serves **4**

75 g (3 oz) **broccoli**, finely
   chopped
75 g (3 oz) **courgettes**, finely
   chopped
75 g (3 oz) mixed red and
   yellow **peppers**, finely
   chopped
25 g (1 oz) **spring onions**,
   finely chopped
40 g (1½ oz) **mushrooms**,
   finely sliced
2 tablespoons **water**
2 tablespoons **pesto**
50 g (2 oz) cooked brown **rice**
50 g (2 oz) cooked wild **rice**
**salt** and **pepper**

**Heat** a large frying pan or wok, add the vegetables
and the measured water and cook over a high heat
for 3–5 minutes, until the vegetables have softened.
Remove from the heat and allow to cool.

**Mix** the cooled vegetables with the pesto and cooked
rice, season well and stir to combine. Cover and chill
until required. Serve topped with a few Parmesan
shavings and some basil leaves, if liked.

**For Mediterranean pasta salad**, cook the vegetables
as above. Meanwhile, cook 150 g (5 oz) macaroni
in lightly salted boiling water until just tender. Mix
4 tablespoons olive oil with 1 tablespoon red wine
vinegar, 1 finely chopped garlic clove, 2 teaspoons
sun-dried tomato paste and a small bunch torn basil
leaves. Season well and toss with the pasta and
the vegetables.

# tandoori chicken salad

Preparation time **15 minutes**,
plus marinating
Finishing time **10 minutes**
Serves **4**

200 g (7 oz) natural **yogurt**
2 tablespoons **lemon** juice
½ teaspoon ground **turmeric**
1 teaspoon **garam masala**
1 teaspoon **cumin** seeds,
  roughly crushed
2 tablespoons **tomato purée**
2 **garlic** cloves, finely chopped
2 cm (¾ inch) piece of fresh
  root **ginger**, finely chopped
3 boneless, skinless **chicken**
  breasts, thickly sliced
1 tablespoon sunflower **oil**

**Salad**
200 g (7 oz) mixed **salad
  leaves**
small bunch of **coriander**
4 tablespoons **lemon juice**

**Mix** the yogurt, lemon juice, spices, tomato purée,
garlic and ginger together in a shallow non-metallic
dish. Add the chicken and toss to coat. Cover and
chill for 3–4 hours or until required.

**When** ready to serve, heat the oil in a large frying pan,
lift the chicken out of the marinade and add a few
pieces at a time to the pan, until all the chicken is in
the pan. Cook over a medium heat for 8–10 minutes
until the chicken is browned and cooked through.

**Meanwhile**, toss the salad leaves and coriander with
the lemon juice and divide between serving plates.
Spoon the chicken on top and serve immediately.

**For tandoori prawn skewers**, thread 400 g (13 oz)
peeled raw tiger prawns on to 8 wooden skewers.
Place in a large shallow china dish and spoon over
the yogurt marinade as above. When ready to serve,
lift out of the marinade and cook under a hot grill for
7–8 minutes, turning until the prawns are bright pink
and cooked through. Serve with salad.

# celeriac remoulade

Preparation time **10 minutes**
Cooking time **4 minutes**
Finishing time **5 minutes**
Serves **4**

500 g (1 lb) **celeriac**, peeled
   and cut into matchsticks
375 g (12 oz) **potatoes**,
   peeled and cut into
   matchsticks
150 ml (¼ pint) **mayonnaise**
150 ml (¼ pint) Greek **yogurt**
1 teaspoon Dijon **mustard**
6 cocktail **gherkins**, finely
   chopped
2 tablespoons **capers**,
   chopped
2 tablespoons chopped
   **tarragon**
1 tablespoon **olive oil**, plus
   extra for drizzling
500 g (1 lb) **asparagus**,
   trimmed
**salt** and **pepper**

**Cook** the celeriac in a saucepan of lightly salted boiling water for 2 minutes until softened. Add the potatoes and cook for a further 2 minutes until just tender. Drain the vegetables and refresh under cold running water. Drain well.

**Meanwhile**, mix together the mayonnaise, yogurt, mustard, gherkins, capers and tarragon in a large bowl, season well and set aside. Add the celeriac and potato and stir well to combine. Cover and chill until required.

**When** ready to serve, heat the oil in a frying pan or griddle pan. Add the asparagus and fry for 2–3 minutes until just beginning to colour.

**Divide** the celeriac and potato remoulade between 4 serving plates. Top with the asparagus spears and serve immediately, drizzled with a little extra olive oil.

**For celeriac remoulade with crispy pancetta & eggs**, make the remoulade as above then chill. When ready to serve, dry-fry 8 rashers of sliced pancetta until crisp. Poach 4 eggs in a saucepan of simmering water until the whites are set and the yolks soft. Lift out of the water with a draining spoon, then serve on a mound of remoulade topped with watercress and the crispy pancetta.

# pâté de campagne

Preparation time **30 minutes**, plus chilling
Cooking time **1¾ hours**
Finishing time **5 minutes**
Serves **6–8**

300 g (10 oz) smoked streaky **bacon**
650 g (1 lb 5 oz) skinned **turkey** leg meat, taken off bone
200 g (7 oz) **chicken livers**
1 **onion**, quartered
375 g (12 oz) **pork** belly, skinned and diced
2–3 **garlic** cloves, finely chopped
small bunch of **thyme**, leaves stripped from stems
6 **cloves**, roughly crushed
6 **juniper** or **allspice** berries, roughly crushed
75 g (3 oz) fresh **breadcrumbs**
75 g (3 oz) ready-to-eat dried **apricots**, diced
3 tablespoons **port**, **Madeira** or **sherry**
**salt** and **pepper**

**Stretch** the rashers of bacon until half as long again, using the blade of a large knife. Use the bacon to cover the base and sides of a 1 kg (2 lb) loaf tin so that the rashers butt together and hang over the top of the tin. Keep back a few rashers for the top.

**Mince** or finely chop the turkey, chicken livers and onion in a food processor then mix in a bowl with the belly pork, garlic, thyme, cloves and juniper or allspice. Stir in the breadcrumbs, apricots and fortified wine. Season well.

**Spoon** the mixture into the bacon-lined tin and press down well. Cover with the remaining bacon, then fold the overhanging rashers over the top. Cover with foil and put the loaf tin in a roasting tin. Pour hot water into the roasting tin to come halfway up the sides of the loaf tin.

**Cook** the pâté in a preheated oven, 160°C (325°F), Gas Mark 3, for 1¾ hours or until the juices run clear when the pâté is pierced with a skewer. Discard the water. Place a small chopping board on top of the pâté and weight down to press it. When cold, chill the pressed pâté overnight.

**When** ready to serve, loosen the pâté and invert on to a chopping board. Cut into thick slices and serve with radishes, salad and crusty bread.

**For brandied duck pâté with pickled walnuts**, omit the turkey and add 500 g (1 lb) skinned diced duck meat, 75 g (3 oz) diced pickled walnuts instead of the apricots, and brandy instead of the fortified wine.

# pan bagna

Preparation time **25 minutes**
Cooking time **15 minutes**
Finishing time **2 minutes**
Serves **4–6**

1 **red pepper**, cored,
  deseeded and quartered
1 **orange pepper**, cored,
  deseeded and quartered
200 g (7 oz) **aubergine**, thinly
  sliced
200 g (7 oz) **courgettes**,
  thickly sliced
5 tablespoons **olive oil**
3 **garlic** cloves, finely chopped
1 round crusty loaf of **bread**,
  20 cm (8 inches) in diameter
2 teaspoons **pesto**
75 g (3 oz) sliced **pastrami** or
  **ham**
150 g (5 oz) **mozzarella**
  cheese, thinly sliced
**salt** and **pepper**

**Arrange** the peppers, skin sides up, in the base of a grill pan then add the aubergines and courgettes in a single layer. Drizzle with 3 tablespoons of the oil, sprinkle with the garlic and season well. Cook under a preheated grill for 10 minutes, turning once. Set aside the courgettes and grill the peppers and aubergine for 5 more minutes until softened and the pepper skins charred. Wrap the peppers in foil and allow to cool.

**Cut** a slice off the top of the loaf then scoop out the centre to leave a case about 2 cm (¾ inch) thick. (Make the soft bread centre into breadcrumbs, stuffing or bread pudding.) Mix the remaining oil with the pesto, season and spoon or brush over the insides of the loaf.

**Skin** the peppers then arrange the orange peppers in the base of the loaf, cover with pastrami or ham, then the courgettes. Add the mozzarella slices, the red peppers and finally the aubergine slices along with any of the cooking juices. Replace the lid of the loaf, wrap in greaseproof paper or foil and keep in a cool place until required. When ready to serve, cut into thick wedges and serve with salad. Ideal for al fresco dining or a picnic.

**For roasted vegetable bread**, roast the vegetables as above then layer in the hollowed-out loaf, adding 75 g (3 oz) sun-dried tomatoes, drained of their oil, and 4 canned artichoke hearts, drained and sliced, instead of the pastrami or ham.

# pomelo & king prawn salad

Preparation time **15 minutes**
Cooking time **2 minutes**
Serves **4**

1 large **pomelo**
125 g (4 oz) **peanuts**, toasted
    and roughly chopped
175 g (6 oz) raw **tiger
    prawns**, peeled
2 tablespoons **grapefruit
    juice**
½ tablespoon **Thai fish sauce**
4 **spring onions**, finely
    shredded
6 **mint** leaves, finely shredded
1 large red **chilli**, finely sliced
pinch of crushed **chilli** or
    **black pepper**
pinch of grated **nutmeg**
4–5 **frisée** or **lollo rosso**
    leaves

**Cut** the pomelo in half and scoop out the segments
and juice. Discard the pith and thick skin surrounding
each segment and break the flesh into small pieces.
Stir the toasted peanuts into the pomelo flesh and set
aside to allow the flavours to blend.

**Cook** the prawns in a saucepan of lightly salted boiling
water for 1–2 minutes, or until the prawns turn pink
and are cooked through. Remove with a slotted spoon
and drain well.

**Add** the prawns to the pomelo flesh with the grapefruit
juice, fish sauce, shredded spring onions and mint.

**Sprinkle** the finely sliced chilli, crushed chilli or pepper
and nutmeg over the salad and toss together. Line the
inside of a bowl with the lettuce leaves and spoon in
the salad. Chill until required.

**For summer pomelo & avocado salad**, cut 1 pomelo
into segments as above. Halve 1 galia melon, deseed,
peel and cut into cubes. Dice ½ cucumber and
3 tomatoes, discarding the seeds. Toss the pomelo,
melon, cucumber and tomato with 3 tablespoons
roughly chopped coriander and leave for 30 minutes.
Just before serving, add 1 peeled, stoned and diced
avocado, if liked, and mix well.

# citrus & pomegranate salad

Preparation time **20 minutes**
Serves **4**

**4 oranges**
2 ruby **grapefruit**
3 small heads of green or
    red-tinged **chicory**
1 **pomegranate**
3 tablespoons **olive oil**
1 tablespoon **honey**
2 tablespoons chopped
    **coriander**
**salt** and **pepper**

**Cut** a slice off the top and bottom of each orange then cut away the pith and skin from the sides with a small serrated knife. Working over a bowl to catch the juices, cut between the membranes to release the flesh and drop the segments into the bowl. Repeat with the grapefruit.

**Separate** the chicory leaves and add to the bowl. Cut the pomegranate in half then pop out the seeds with the point of a small knife, or flex the skin.

**To** make the dressing, beat the oil, honey, coriander leaves and seasoning together then toss with the fruit and chicory. Chill until ready to serve.

**Stir** the fruit salad and spoon into shallow dishes. Serve with warm crusty bread, if liked.

**For peppered citrus & strawberry salad**, mix the oranges and the grapefruit with 250 g (8 oz) halved strawberries. Toss in the dressing as above, omitting the coriander and adding ¼ teaspoon roughly crushed peppercorns instead.

# tortilla with romesco sauce

Preparation time **25 minutes**
Cooking time **22–24 minutes**
Finishing time **2 minutes**
Serves **4**

2 tablespoons **olive oil**
625 g (1¼ lb) **potatoes**, thinly
  sliced
1 **onion,** halved and thinly
  sliced
2 **garlic** cloves, finely chopped
  (optional)
8 **eggs**
2 tablespoons **water**
**salt** and **pepper**

**Romesco sauce**
1 **onion**, chopped
1 tablespoon **olive oil**
2 **garlic** cloves, finely chopped
4 **tomatoes**, skinned and
  diced
½ teaspoon smoked **paprika**
40 g (1½ oz) blanched
  **almonds,** toasted and finely
  chopped

**Heat** the oil in a large non-stick frying pan, add the potatoes, onion and garlic, if using, cover and fry gently for 15 minutes, stirring from time to time until the potatoes are tender.

**Meanwhile**, make the sauce. Fry the onion in the oil in a saucepan for 5 minutes until just beginning to brown. Add the garlic, tomatoes and paprika and cook for 2 minutes. Stir in the almonds, season and simmer for 10 minutes until thick.

**Beat** the eggs, measured water and some seasoning together. Pour into the frying pan with the potatoes and cook for 4–5 minutes without stirring, until the base is golden and the top almost set. Transfer the pan to a hot grill and cook the top of the tortilla for 4–5 minutes until browned and set. Loosen the edges of the tortilla and turn out on to a plate. Leave in a cool place until required.

**When** ready to serve, cut the tortilla into wedges and arrange on small serving plates with spoonfuls of the sauce and a few olives, if liked.

**For courgette frittata with romesco sauce**, heat the oil in the frying pan then add 1 thinly sliced red onion and 500 g (1 lb) diced courgettes. Fry gently for 5 minutes until just tender. Beat the 8 eggs with 2 tablespoons water, 3 tablespoons chopped mint and season well. Add to the pan and finish as above. Serve warm or cold with the romesco sauce flavoured with 2 tablespoons chopped mint.

# sweet potato & haloumi salad

Preparation time **10 minutes**
Cooking time **2 minutes**
Finishing time **10 minutes**
Serves **4**

500 g (1 lb) **sweet potatoes**,
 sliced
3 tablespoons **olive oil**
250 g (8 oz) **haloumi** cheese,
 thinly sliced
75 g (3 oz) **rocket** leaves

**Dressing**
5 tablespoons **olive oil**
3 tablespoons runny **honey**
2 tablespoons **lemon or lime
 juice**
1½ teaspoons **black onion**
 seeds
1 red **chilli**, deseeded and
 finely sliced
2 teaspoons chopped **lemon
 thyme**
**salt** and **pepper**

**Mix** together all the ingredients for the dressing in a small bowl. Set aside until required.

**Cook** the sweet potatoes in a saucepan of lightly salted boiling water for 2 minutes. Drain well and chill until required.

**When** ready to serve, heat the oil in a large frying pan, add the sweet potatoes and fry for about 10 minutes, turning once, until golden.

**Meanwhile**, place the haloumi slices on a lightly oiled foil-lined grill rack. Cook under a preheated moderate grill for about 3 minutes until golden.

**Divide** the sweet potatoes, cheese and rocket between 4 serving plates and spoon over the dressing. Serve immediately.

# tabbouleh with fruit & nuts

Preparation time **15 minutes**, plus soaking
Serves **4**

150 g (5 oz) **bulgar wheat**
75 g (3 oz) unsalted, shelled **pistachio nuts**
1 small red **onion**, finely chopped
3 **garlic** cloves, crushed
25 g (1 oz) flat-leaf **parsley**, chopped
15 g (½ oz) **mint**, chopped
finely grated rind and juice of 1 **lemon**
150 g (5 oz) ready-to-eat **prunes**, sliced
4 tablespoons **olive oil**
**salt** and **pepper**

**Place** the bulgar wheat in a bowl, cover with plenty of boiling water and leave to soak for 15 minutes.

**Mix** the nuts with the onion, garlic, parsley, mint, lemon rind and juice and prunes in a large bowl.

**Drain** the bulgar wheat thoroughly in a sieve, pressing out as much moisture as possible with the back of a spoon. Add to the other ingredients with the oil and season to taste with salt and pepper. Toss the ingredients to mix well, then chill until required.

**For couscous tabbouleh with harissa**, soak 175 g (6 oz) couscous, 50 g (2 oz) raisins and 50 g (2 oz) chopped stoned dates in 300 ml (½ pint) boiling water for 5 minutes. Mix 3 tablespoons olive oil with 1 teaspoon harissa paste, and stir into the couscous with 1 chopped red onion, a handful of chopped coriander and 2 chopped tomatoes.

# leeks milanese

Preparation time **25 minutes**
Cooking time **10 minutes**
Finishing time **2 minutes**
Serves **4**

6 tablespoons **olive oil**
100 g (3½ oz) **ciabatta** or
　rustic white **bread**, torn into
　pieces
1 **garlic** clove, finely chopped
12 baby **leeks**
2 **eggs**, hard boiled and
　roughly chopped
1 tablespoon red wine
　**vinegar**
1 teaspoon Dijon **mustard**
1 tablespoon **capers**
3 tablespoons roughly
　chopped flat-leaf **parsley**
**salt** and **pepper**

**Heat** 2 tablespoons of the oil in a frying pan, add the bread and garlic and fry until crisp and golden. Transfer to a plate and allow to cool. Cover and set aside.

**Cut** the leeks into 2 or 3 slices, depending on their length, then steam them over a pan of boiling water for 3–4 minutes until just tender. Arrange the leeks in a salad bowl and sprinkle the chopped eggs over the top.

**Beat** the remaining oil with the vinegar, mustard and seasoning. Drizzle over the leeks and add the capers and parsley. Cover and chill until required.

**When** ready to serve, toss the salad gently and sprinkle with the croûtons. Spoon on to serving plates and serve immediately.

**For milanese pasta salad**, cook 300 g (10 oz) of pasta shells in boiling water until just tender, adding 150 g (5 oz) of broccoli florets for the last 3 minutes. Drain the pasta and toss with the dressing, eggs, capers and parsley, as above. Sprinkle with the croûtons and serve immediately with a little grated Parmesan.

# asian tuna salad

Preparation time **15 minutes**
Finishing time **2 minutes**
Serves **4**

350 g (11½ oz) **tuna steak**,
  cut into strips
3 tablespoons **soy sauce**
1 teaspoon **wasabi paste**
1 tablespoon **sake** or dry
  white **wine**
200 g (7 oz) mixed **salad
  leaves**
150 g (5 oz) baby yellow
  **tomatoes,** halved
1 **cucumber,** sliced into wide
  fine strips

**Dressing**
2 tablespoons **soy sauce**
1 tablespoon **lime juice**
1 teaspoon brown **sugar**
2 teaspoons **sesame oil**

**Combine** the tuna strips with the soy sauce, wasabi and sake. Cover and chill until required.

**Arrange** the salad leaves, tomatoes and cucumber on a large serving plate. Cover and chill until required. Mix the dressing ingredients in a bowl and set aside.

**When** ready to serve, heat a non-stick pan over a high heat and fry the tuna strips for about 10 seconds on each side, or until seared. Arrange the tuna on top of the salad, drizzle with the dressing and serve immediately.

**For asian pork salad**, thinly slice 350 g (12 oz) pork tenderloin instead of the tuna. Marinate in the soy mixture as above and make the salad. Fry the pork in a heated ridged frying pan for 5–6 minutes, turning once or twice until cooked through. Serve on the salad drizzled with the dressing.

# everyday suppers

# pork goujons with chips

Preparation time **25 minutes**
Cooking time **10 minutes**
Finishing time **8 minutes**
Serves **4**

500 g (1 lb) **pork** escalopes
  or trimmed loin steaks
3 tablespoons plain **flour**
1 teaspoon **paprika**
small bunch of **thyme**, leaves
  stripped from stems
100 g (3½ oz) fresh
  **breadcrumbs**
finely grated rind of 1 **lemon**
2 **eggs**
1 **onion**, chopped
1 tablespoon sunflower **oil**,
  plus extra for shallow frying
2 **garlic** cloves, finely chopped
400 g (13 oz) can chopped
  **tomatoes**
**salt** and **pepper**

**Place** the pork between two sheets of clingfilm and beat with a rolling pin until half the original thickness. Cut the pork into thick strips.

**Mix** the flour, paprika, three-quarters of the thyme leaves and a little seasoning on a plate. Put the breadcrumbs and lemon rind on a second plate and beat the eggs in a large shallow dish. Coat the pork strips one at a time in the flour, then the egg, and then roll in the breadcrumbs. Put in a single layer on a baking sheet, cover and chill until required.

**Fry** the onion in the oil for 5 minutes until just beginning to brown, stir in the garlic then the tomatoes, a little thyme and some seasoning. Simmer for 5 minutes until thickened and set aside.

**When** ready to serve, heat a thin layer of oil in a frying pan, add the pork strips and fry in batches for 2 minutes each side or until golden brown and cooked through. Warm the sauce through then arrange the pork on serving plates with spoonfuls of sauce, lemon wedges and chunky chips.

**For cheesy chicken goujons**, use the same weight of boneless, skinless chicken breasts and prepare in the same way as the pork. Omit the thyme and lemon rind, instead mixing 25 g (1 oz) finely grated Parmesan with the breadcrumbs.

# piccadillo tortillas

Preparation time **25 minutes**
Cooking time **about 1 hour**
Finishing time **15 minutes**
Serves **4**

250 g (8 oz) minced **pork**
250 g (8 oz) minced **beef**
1 **onion**, chopped
2 **garlic** cloves, finely chopped
1 teaspoon smoked **paprika**
1 teaspoon ground **cumin**
½ teaspoon ground **cinnamon**
2 tablespoons flaked **almonds**
2 tablespoons red wine
  **vinegar**
50 g (2 oz) **raisins**
400 g (13 oz) can chopped
  **tomatoes**
300 ml (½ pint) **chicken stock**

**Salsa**
1 **red pepper**, cored,
  deseeded and chopped
½ red **onion**, finely chopped
small bunch of **coriander**,
  finely chopped

8 large soft flour **tortillas**
200 ml (7 fl oz) **crème fraîche**
**salt** and **pepper**

**Dry-fry** the minced pork and beef in a flameproof casserole dish with the onion for 5 minutes, stirring until the mince is evenly browned.

**Stir** in the garlic, paprika, cumin and cinnamon then mix in the almonds, vinegar, raisins and tomatoes. Add the stock and some seasoning and bring to the boil, stirring occasionally. Cover and cook in a preheated oven, 180°C (350°F), Gas Mark 4, for 1 hour. Allow to cool, then chill until required.

**To** make the salsa, mix together the red pepper, red onion and coriander in a bowl and chill until required.

**When** ready to serve, reheat the piccadillo on the hob for 15 minutes, stirring until piping hot. Warm the tortillas according to the instructions on the packet. Divide the piccadillo between the tortillas, and top with spoonfuls of crème fraîche and salsa. Roll up and serve immediately.

**For chillied tortillas**, use 500 g (1 lb) minced beef instead of a mixture of pork and beef. Add 1 large dried red chilli, broken in two, and a 400 g (13 oz) can of red kidney beans instead of the almonds and raisins. Cook and serve as above.

# spinach & feta filo pie

Preparation time **20 minutes**
Cooking time about **1 hour**
Serves **6**

750 g (1 1/2 lb) fresh **spinach**
    leaves, rinsed
250 g (8 oz) **feta** cheese,
    roughly crumbled
1/2 teaspoon dried **chilli flakes**
75 g (3 oz) **Parmesan**
    cheese, finely grated
50 g (2 oz) **pine nuts**, toasted
15 g (1/2 oz) **dill**, chopped
15 g (1/2 oz) **tarragon**,
    chopped
3 **eggs**, beaten
pinch of grated **nutmeg**
250 g (8 oz) **filo pastry**
5–8 tablespoons **olive oil**
1 tablespoon **sesame** seeds
**salt** and **pepper**

**Cook** the spinach in a large saucepan, with just the water left on the leaves after rinsing, over a low heat until wilted and soft. Drain well pressing out the juices.

**Mix** the feta into the spinach with the chilli flakes, Parmesan, pine nuts and herbs. Mix in the beaten eggs with plenty of salt, pepper and grated nutmeg.

**Unwrap** the filo pastry and, working quickly, brush the top sheet of pastry with a little olive oil. Lay in the bottom of a lightly greased 20 cm (8 inch) loose-bottomed cake tin with the edges overlapping the rim of the tin. Brush the next sheet of pastry and lay it in the opposite direction to cover the base of the tin. Repeat with 4–6 sheets of pastry, saving 3 sheets to make a lid.

**Spoon** the spinach mixture into the filo pastry shell, pushing it in with the back of the spoon and to level.

**Cut** the remaining pastry into 5 cm (2 inch) wide strips. One by one, brush them with oil and place them on top of the spinach in a casual folded arrangement. Fold the overhanging filo towards the middle of the pie, sprinkle with sesame seeds and bake in a preheated oven, 190°C (375°F), Gas Mark 5, for 50–60 minutes. Leave to cool. When ready to serve, remove from the tin and serve with salad.

**For aubergine & almond filo pie**, fill the pie with 3 sliced and fried aubergines layered with 375 g (12 oz) sliced tomatoes, sprinkled with 3 chopped garlic cloves, 4 tablespoons ground almonds, a little ground allspice and salt and pepper. Cook as above, covering with foil if the pie becomes too brown.

# bacon & oat-topped mackerel

Preparation time **15 minutes**
Finishing time **10 minutes**
Serves **4**

4 **mackerel**, heads removed,
  boned
4 teaspoons finely chopped
  **rosemary** leaves
2 rashers of smoked back
  **bacon**, finely diced
6 tablespoons porridge **oats**
40 g (1 ½ oz) **walnuts**, roughly
  chopped
finely grated rind and juice of
  1 **lemon**
2 tablespoons **olive oil**
2 teaspoons hot **horseradish**
6 tablespoons Greek **yogurt**
**salt** and **pepper**

**Arrange** the mackerel fillets skin side down on a baking sheet lined with oiled baking paper or foil.

**Mix** the rosemary, bacon, oats, walnuts and lemon rind together, season then spoon on top of the fish. Drizzle with the lemon juice and oil. Cover and chill until required.

**Mix** the horseradish and yogurt in a small bowl with a little seasoning, cover and chill until required.

**When** ready to serve, remove the cover and bake the mackerel in a preheated oven, 220°C (425°F), Gas Mark 7, for 10 minutes until the topping is crisp and golden and the fish flakes easily when pressed with a knife. Serve with salad and the horseradish sauce.

**For baked mackerel with a herb crust**, tear 50 g (2 oz) ciabatta or other rustic bread into small pieces and toss with 3 tablespoons chopped chives. Season and mix with the grated rind and juice of 1 lemon and 2 tablespoons olive oil. Spoon over the mackerel and bake as above. Serve with 150 g (5 oz) natural yogurt mixed with 2 teaspoons wholegrain mustard and 1 teaspoon honey.

# pork skewers with parsnip mash

Preparation time **20 minutes**
Cooking time **15 minutes**
Finishing time **10 minutes**
Serves **4**

750 g (1½ lb) **parsnips**, cut into chunks

2 sharp dessert **apples**, such as Granny Smith or Braeburn, peeled, cored and chopped

40 g (1½ oz) **butter**

2 tablespoons **olive oil**

2 tablespoons red wine **vinegar**

1 tablespoon runny **honey**

2 teaspoons **fennel** seeds, roughly crushed

625 g (1¼ lb) **pork** tenderloin, cubed

16 fresh **bay** leaves (optional)

**salt** and **pepper**

**Cook** the parsnips in a saucepan of boiling water for 10 minutes. Add the apples and cook for 5 more minutes or until the apples and parsnips are tender. Drain and mash the parsnips and apples with the butter and a little seasoning. Allow to cool, spoon into a microwave-proof serving dish, cover with clingfilm and chill until required.

**Meanwhile**, make the marinade by mixing the oil, vinegar, honey and fennel seeds with a little seasoning in a shallow non-metallic dish. Add the pork and toss together. Cover and chill until required.

**When** ready to serve, thread the pork cubes and bay leaves, if using, on to 8 skewers. Arrange in a grill pan and cook under a preheated medium grill for 10 minutes, turning once or twice and spooning the marinade over until the pork is caramelized and cooked through.

**Reheat** the mash by piercing the clingfilm and cooking in a microwave on full power for 3–4 minutes until piping hot. Alternatively, return to a small saucepan and heat gently, stirring constantly, until hot. Spoon on to plates, top with the skewers and drizzle the pan juices over the top. Serve with steamed green beans, if liked.

**For chicken skewers with sweet potato mash**, omit the fennel seeds from the marinade and add 1 teaspoon Cajun spices. Add 625 g (1¼ lb) boneless skinless chicken breasts cut into cubes. When ready to serve, thread the chicken cubes on to 8 skewers and grill as above. Serve with 875 g (1¾ lb) sweet potatoes that have been cooked and mashed.

# green chicken kebabs

Preparation time **15 minutes**
Finishing time **10–12 minutes**
Serves **4**

100 ml (3½ fl oz) natural
  **yogurt**
2 **garlic** cloves, crushed
2 teaspoons finely grated
  fresh root **ginger**
2 teaspoons ground **cumin**
1 teaspoon ground **coriander**
1 green **chilli**, deseeded and
  finely chopped
large handful of chopped
  **coriander**
small handful of chopped **mint**
4 tablespoons **lime juice**
4 skinless, boneless **chicken**
  breasts, cubed
**salt**

**Place** the yogurt, garlic, ginger, cumin, ground coriander, chilli, chopped herbs and lime juice in a blender or food processor and blend until fairly smooth. Season lightly.

**Place** the chicken in a large mixing bowl, pour over the spice mixture and toss to coat evenly. Cover and chill until required.

**When** ready to cook, thread the chicken pieces on to 8 bamboo skewers. Cook under a preheated medium-hot grill for 8–10 minutes, turning frequently, until cooked through and lightly browned. Serve immediately with a cucumber salad, with lime wedges for squeezing.

**For green cod steaks**, mix all the ingredients above together except the chicken and the yogurt. Use the mixture to coat four 175 g (6 oz) cod steaks. Drizzle with 2 tablespoons olive oil and chill until required. Bake in a preheated oven, 190°C (375°F), Gas Mark 5, for 15–18 minutes or until the fish flakes when pressed with a knife.

# lamb ragu with toasted walnuts

Preparation time **15 minutes**
Cooking time **1 hour
35 minutes**
Finishing time **10 minutes**
Serves **4**

1 tablespoon **olive oil**
500 g (1 lb) diced **lamb**
1 **onion**, chopped
2 **garlic** cloves, finely chopped
50 g (2 oz) **walnut** pieces,
plus extra to garnish
1 tablespoon plain **flour**
450 ml (¾ pint) **lamb stock**
200 ml (7 fl oz) **red wine**
2 tablespoons **tomato purée**
1 **bouquet garni**
250 g (8 oz) **rigatoni** or
**penne**
handful of chopped flat-leaf
**parsley**
**salt** and **pepper**

**Heat** the oil in a flameproof casserole, add the lamb a few pieces at a time, then add the onion. Fry for about 5 minutes, stirring until browned all over.

**Add** the garlic and walnuts and fry for a couple of minutes more until the nuts are lightly toasted. Stir in the flour then add the stock, wine, tomato purée, bouquet garni and a little seasoning. Bring to the boil, stirring occasionally. Cover and cook in a preheated oven, 160°C (325°F), Gas Mark 3, for 1½ hours or until the lamb is tender. Allow to cool then chill until required.

**When** ready to serve, cook the pasta in a large saucepan of boiling water for 8–10 minutes until just tender. Reheat the lamb on the hob, stirring until piping hot. Drain the pasta then toss with the lamb and sprinkle with chopped parsley and a few extra walnuts. Spoon into shallow bowls. Serve with a salad of rocket, watercress and spinach dressed with lemon juice and sprinkled with Parmesan shavings.

**For lamb daube**, use 75 g (3 oz) diced smoked streaky bacon or pancetta instead of the walnuts. Add 75 g (3 oz) pitted prunes with the bouquet garni. Cook as above. Serve with mashed potatoes.

# souvlaki burgers

Preparation time **25 minutes**
Finishing time **10 minutes**
Serves **4**

500 g (1 lb) lean minced **lamb**
small bunch of **coriander**,
    roughly chopped
1 red **onion**, halved and thinly
    sliced
1 tablespoon **coriander** seeds
1 teaspoon **cumin** seeds
1 **garlic** clove
small bunch of **mint**
6 tablespoons Greek **yogurt**
4 soft floury **burger buns**
2 Little Gem **lettuces**
**salt** and **pepper**

**Put** the lamb, chopped coriander and half the onion into a food processor bowl. Tip the seeds into a pestle and mortar and grind roughly. Add all but 1 teaspoon to the mince mixture, season then blitz together. Alternatively, finely chop half the onion and coriander then mix into the mince with the spices.

**Shape** the lamb mixture into 4 thick burgers, arrange on a baking sheet, cover and chill until required. Wrap the remaining sliced onions and chill until required.

**Crush** the garlic and mint together in a pestle and mortar, add the remaining crushed seeds, the yogurt and some pepper. Spoon into a small dish, cover and chill until required.

**When** ready to serve, grill or barbecue the burgers for about 10 minutes, turning once or twice until browned and cooked right through. Slit and toast the cut sides of the rolls then add the lettuce, burgers, spoonfuls of the yogurt mix and the remaining onions. Serve with chunky chips, if liked.

**For Greek lamb souvlaki**, put the minced lamb, coriander and red onion in a food processor as above then add 1 large mild, deseeded and finely chopped red chilli. Divide the mixture into 8, shape into sausage shapes around 8 metal skewers, and chill until required. Grill the koftas for 10 minutes until browned and cooked through. Serve in 4 warmed pitta breads, with salad and tzatiki made with 6 tablespoons Greek yogurt mixed with ½ diced cucumber and 2 tablespoons chopped coriander.

# chicken & chorizo pappadelle

Preparation time **15 minutes**
Cooking time **35 minutes**
Finishing time **10 minutes**
Serves **4**

2 tablespoons **olive oil**
6 skinless, boneless **chicken**
   thighs, cut into chunks
1 **onion**, chopped
125 g (4 oz) **chorizo**, skinned
   and diced
2 **garlic** cloves, finely chopped
400 g (13 oz) can chopped
   **tomatoes**
200 ml (7 fl oz) **chicken stock**
1 tablespoon **capers**
375 g (12 oz) **pappadelle** or
   **tagliatelle**
50 g (2 oz) pitted mixed
   **olives**
small bunch of **basil**, torn
**salt** and **pepper**

**Heat** the oil in a saucepan, add the diced chicken and onion and fry for 5 minutes, stirring until golden. Add the chorizo and garlic and cook for 2 minutes.

**Mix** in the tomatoes, stock, capers and seasoning, bring to the boil then cover and cook gently for 30 minutes, stirring from time to time, until the sauce has thickened slightly and the chicken is cooked through. Allow to cool then chill until required.

**When** ready to serve, cook the pasta in a large saucepan of boiling water for 7–9 minutes until just tender. Meanwhile, add the olives and half the basil to the chicken and reheat thoroughly until piping hot. Drain the pasta, toss with the chicken mixture then spoon into dishes and garnish with the remaining basil leaves.

**For chicken & sausage pasta**, omit the chorizo, capers and olives and add instead 3 sliced cooked sausages. Toss with 375 g (12 oz) cooked pasta shells and some chopped sage leaves.

# beetroot chilli & papaya salsa

Preparation time **15 minutes**
Cooking time **1 hour
35 minutes**
Finishing time **10 minutes**
Serves **4**

1 tablespoon sunflower **oil**
1 **onion**, chopped
2 **garlic** cloves, finely chopped
500 g (1 lb) raw **beetroot**,
  peeled and cubed
400 g (13 oz) can red **kidney
  beans**, drained
1–2 teaspoons dried **chilli
  flakes**, to taste
2 teaspoons **paprika**
1 teaspoon ground **cinnamon**
400 g (13 oz) can chopped
  **tomatoes**
450 ml (¾ pint) **vegetable
  stock**
2 tablespoons red wine **vinegar**
1 tablespoon brown **sugar**
1 **papaya**, peeled, deseeded
  and diced
½ small red **onion**, finely
  chopped
1 **tomato**, deseeded and diced
small bunch of **coriander**,
  roughly chopped
**salt** and **pepper**
**soured cream**

**Heat** the oil in a flameproof casserole, add the onion and fry for 5 minutes until lightly browned. Mix in the garlic, beetroot, kidney beans, chilli flakes and spices, then add the tomatoes, stock, vinegar, sugar and plenty of seasoning.

**Bring** to the boil then cover and cook in a preheated oven, 180°C (350°F), Gas Mark 4, for 1½ hours or until the beetroot is tender. Allow to cool then chill until required.

**To** make the salsa, mix together the papaya, red onion, tomato and coriander and spoon into a serving dish. Cover and chill until required.

**When** ready to serve, reheat the chilli on the hob, topping up with extra stock if needed, and stirring frequently until piping hot. Spoon into bowls and top with spoonfuls of the salsa, and some soured cream. Serve with brown rice or warmed tortillas.

**For beetroot, chilli & orange salad**, stir the grated rind and juice of 1 orange into the cooked and cooled beetroot mixture. Spoon on to lettuce leaves and top with low-fat natural yogurt sprinkled with mint leaves and extra orange segments.

# feta-stuffed peppers

Preparation time **20 minutes**
Cooking time **10 minutes**
Finishing time **30 minutes**
Serves **4**

150 g (5 oz) **bulgar wheat**
800 ml (1 pint 7 fl oz)
  **vegetable stock**
2 **orange peppers**
2 **yellow peppers**
40 g (1½ oz) **sultanas**
¼ teaspoon ground **allspice**
100 g (3½ oz) **feta** cheese,
  crumbled
small bunch of **basil**, torn
1 **onion**, chopped
3 tablespoons **olive oil**
3 **garlic** cloves, finely chopped
500 g (1 lb) **tomatoes**,
  roughly chopped
**salt** and **pepper**

**Cook** the bulgar wheat in 600 ml (1 pint) of the stock in a covered saucepan for 10 minutes.

**Lay** each pepper on a chopping board and make a cut from the base up towards and around the stem, opening out enough to remove the core and seeds but not so much that the pepper splits in two.

**Drain** off any excess stock from the cooked bulgar, add the sultanas, allspice, feta, a little of the basil and some seasoning. Mix together and spoon into the peppers. Transfer to a roasting tin.

**Fry** the onion in 1 tablespoon of the oil for 5 minutes until lightly browned. Add the garlic, tomatoes, remaining stock and a little seasoning. Spoon around the peppers, sprinkle with a little more torn basil then leave to cool. Cover and chill until required.

**When** ready to serve, drizzle the peppers with the remaining oil and cook in a preheated oven, 200°C (400°F), Gas Mark 6, for 30 minutes or until the peppers are softened. Spoon into shallow bowls and garnish with the remaining basil.

**For bulgar & feta salad**, make up the stuffing with the cooked bulgar, sultanas, allspice, feta and a small handful of torn basil leaves. Mix 3 tablespoons olive oil, 1 tablespoon red wine vinegar, and 1 finely chopped garlic clove with salt and pepper. Stir into the bulgar mixture with 4 diced tomatoes and 4 chopped spring onions. Chill until required.

# smoked haddock fishcakes

Preparation time **30 minutes**
Cooking time **15 minutes**
Finishing time **16–20 minutes**
Serves **4**

625 g (1 ¼ lb) **potatoes**, cut
   into chunks
500 g (1 lb) **smoked haddock**
4 **eggs**
25 g (1 oz) **butter**
2–3 tablespoons **milk**
3 tablespoons chopped
   **chives** or **parsley**
2 tablespoons **water**
125 g (4 oz) fresh
   **breadcrumbs**
4 tablespoons sunflower **oil**
**salt** and **pepper**

**Tartare sauce**
200 ml (7 fl oz) **crème fraîche**
finely grated rind of 1 **lemon**
2 tablespoons chopped
   **chives** or **parsley**
3 teaspoons **capers**, roughly
   chopped
50 g (2 oz) **gherkins**, finely
   chopped

**Half-fill** the base of a steamer with water and bring to the boil. Cook the potatoes in the water in the base for 15 minutes or until tender, and the fish in the top for 8–10 minutes until it flakes when pressed with a knife. Hard-boil 2 of the eggs for 8 minutes.

**Skin** and flake the fish, discarding any bones. Shell and roughly chop the hard-boiled eggs. Drain and mash the potatoes with the butter, milk and seasoning. Stir the fish, chopped egg and chopped herbs into the mash. Divide into 8 portions and pat into thick rounds.

**Beat** the remaining eggs in a shallow dish with the measured water. Put the breadcrumbs in a second shallow dish. Coat the fishcakes in egg on both sides, then coat in the breadcrumbs. Arrange on a baking sheet, cover and chill until required.

**Mix** all the sauce ingredients with a little seasoning. Spoon into a serving dish, cover and chill until required.

**When** ready to serve, heat half the oil in a frying pan, add 4 fishcakes, cover and fry over a medium heat for 8–10 minutes, turning once, until golden on both sides and hot through. Keep hot in the oven while cooking the remaining cakes in the remaining oil. Serve with spoonfuls of sauce, lemon wedges and a green salad.

**For salmon & prawn fishcakes**, use 500 g (1 lb) salmon fillet instead of the smoked haddock, adding 150 g (5 oz) roughly chopped cooked prawns in place of the hard-boiled eggs. Continue as above and serve with lemon mayonnaise.

# beery beef with cheesy dumplings

Preparation time **25 minutes**
Cooking time **1 hour**
  **35 minutes**
Finishing time **20 minutes**
Serves **4**

1 tablespoon sunflower **oil**
675 g (1 lb 6 oz) stewing
  **beef**, diced
1 **onion**, roughly chopped
1 tablespoon plain **flour**
250 ml (8 fl oz) **beer** or
  **light ale**
750 ml (1 ¼ pints) **beef stock**
2 tablespoons **Worcestershire
  sauce**
1 tablespoon wholegrain
  **mustard**
2 **carrots**, diced
2 **parsnips**, diced
½ small **swede**, diced

**Dumplings**
125 g (4 oz) self-raising **flour**
50 g (2 oz) vegetable **suet**
75 g (3 oz) mature **Cheddar**
  cheese, grated
2 teaspoons wholegrain
  **mustard**
4–5 tablespoons **water**
**salt** and **pepper**

**Heat** the oil in a flameproof casserole and add the beef a few pieces at a time. Cook for a few minutes, then add the onion and fry over a high heat, stirring, until the meat is evenly browned.

**Stir** in the plain flour, then mix in the beer, 600 ml (1 pint) of the stock, the Worcestershire sauce, mustard and vegetables. Season and bring to the boil, stirring occasionally. Cover the dish and cook in a preheated oven, 160°C (325°F), Gas Mark 3, for 1 ½ hours or until the meat and vegetables are tender. Allow to cool then chill until required.

**Mix** the self-raising flour, suet, two-thirds of the cheese and a little seasoning in a bowl, cover and set aside.

**When** ready to serve, stir the mustard and enough water into the dumpling mix to make a soft smooth dough. Shape into 8 balls with floured hands. Bring the beef casserole back to the boil on the hob, adding the remaining stock, if needed. Stir well and add the dumplings, leaving space between them. Cover and simmer for 15 minutes until the dumplings are fluffy.

**Sprinkle** the dumplings with the remaining cheese then transfer the casserole to a preheated hot grill to melt and brown the cheese topping. Spoon into shallow bowls and serve immediately.

**For lamb stew with rosemary dumplings**, swap the beef for lamb, beer for dry cider, beef stock for chicken stock, and Worcestershire sauce and mustard for a few stems of fresh rosemary. For the dumplings, use 2 tablespoons of chopped rosemary leaves instead of the cheese and mustard.

# tricolore cauliflower gratin

Preparation time **15 minutes**
Cooking time **12 minutes**
Finishing time **20 minutes**
Serves **4**

3 **tomatoes**, sliced
200 g (7 oz) fresh **spinach** leaves
pinch of grated **nutmeg**
1 **cauliflower**, cut into florets
40 g (1½ oz) **butter**
40 g (1½ oz) plain **flour**
450 ml (¾ pint) semi-skimmed **milk**
175 g (6 oz) mature **Cheddar** cheese, grated
½ slice of **bread**, torn into tiny pieces
2 tablespoons **sunflower** seeds
2 tablespoons **pumpkin** seeds
**salt** and **pepper**

**Arrange** the tomatoes in the base of shallow ovenproof dish. Steam the spinach for 1–2 minutes until just wilted and spoon over the tomatoes. Sprinkle with a little nutmeg and some seasoning.

**Steam** the cauliflower for 8–10 minutes until just tender. Meanwhile, melt the butter in a separate saucepan and stir in the flour. Gradually whisk in the milk and bring to the boil, stirring constantly, until smooth and thick. Stir in two-thirds of the cheese and season well.

**Arrange** the cauliflower on top of the spinach, then gently mix together. Pour the sauce over the top. Mix the remaining cheese with the torn bread and seeds then sprinkle over the cheese sauce. Allow to cool, cover and chill until required.

**When** ready to serve, remove the cover and cook in a preheated oven, 200°C (400°F), Gas Mark 6, for 20 minutes until the topping is crisp and golden and the vegetables are piping hot.

**For classic cauliflower cheese**, make the cheese sauce as above, omitting the nutmeg and stir in 1 teaspoon English mustard. Cut 1 large cauliflower into florets and cook in a saucepan of boiling water for 8–10 minutes or until tender and drain well. Mix the cauliflower with the sauce, tip into a shallow dish, sprinkle with a little extra grated cheese and 2 tablespoons fine breadcrumbs, then grill until golden. Serve with halved grilled tomatoes drizzled with balsamic vinegar.

# fish pie

Preparation time **30 minutes**
Cooking time **15 minutes**
Finishing time **40–45 minutes**
Serves **4**

375 g (12 oz) **salmon** fillet
375 g (12 oz) **cod** loin
600 ml (1 pint) semi-skimmed
  **milk**
1 **bay** leaf
1 **leek**, thinly sliced
625 g (1¼ lb) **potatoes**, thinly
  sliced
3 tablespoons chopped **dill**
50 g (2 oz) **butter**
50 g (2 oz) **plain flour**
100 g (3½ oz) mature
  **Cheddar** cheese, grated
**salt** and **pepper**

**Put** the salmon and cod into a frying pan, pour over enough of the milk to just cover it, then add the bay leaf and a little seasoning. Bring to the boil then cover and simmer for 8 minutes until the fish flakes when pressed with a knife, adding the leeks for the last 2 minutes.

**Meanwhile**, cook the potatoes in a saucepan of boiling water for 3–4 minutes until just tender. Drain, rinse in cold water and drain again.

**Lift** the fish out of the milk and flake the flesh into large pieces, discarding the skin and any bones. Transfer to a 1.2 litre (2 pint), 5 cm (2 inch) deep ovenproof dish. Strain the milk into a jug containing the remaining milk and discard the bay leaf. Arrange the leeks on top of the fish and sprinkle with the dill.

**Heat** the butter in a clean pan, stir in the flour then gradually whisk in the milk. Bring to the boil, whisking until thickened and smooth. Season and stir in three-quarters of the cheese. Pour half the sauce over the fish. Arrange the potato slices overlapping on top, pour over the remaining sauce, then sprinkle with the remaining cheese. Allow to cool, then chill until required.

**When** ready to serve, remove the cover and cook the fish pie in a preheated oven, 180°C (350°F), Gas Mark 4, for 40–45 minutes until the top is golden brown and the pie is piping hot. Serve with green beans, if liked.

**For smoked haddock & bacon pie**, poach 625 g (1¼ lb) smoked haddock in the milk as above. Grill 125 g (4 oz) back bacon until crispy, then chop it roughly and add to the pie with 3 tablespoons chopped chives. Finish as above.

# prawn & fennel thai curry

Preparation time **15 minutes**
Cooking time **7–8 minutes**
Finishing time **9–10 minutes**
Serves **4**

1 **onion**, quartered
2.5 cm (1 inch) piece of fresh
  **root ginger**, peeled and
  quartered
2 **garlic** cloves
1 mild red **chilli**, halved and
  deseeded
1 tablespoon sunflower **oil**
1 tablespoon **Thai green
  curry paste**
400 ml (13 fl oz) can reduced-
  fat **coconut milk**
300 ml (½ pint) **fish stock**
2 teaspoons **Thai fish sauce**
75 g (3 oz) fine rice **noodles**
1 **fennel** bulb, roughly
  chopped
100 g (3½ oz) **green beans**,
  thickly sliced
small bunch of **coriander**
75 g (3 oz) baby **corn cobs**,
  thickly sliced
300 g (10 oz) peeled cooked
  **prawns**

**Blitz** the onion, ginger, garlic and chilli in a blender
or food processor to form a rough paste. Alternatively,
chop the ingredients very finely by hand. Heat the oil
in a saucepan, add the onion paste and fry for
2–3 minutes, stirring, until softened.

**Stir** in the curry paste and cook briefly, then mix in the
coconut milk, fish stock and fish sauce. Simmer gently
for 5 minutes. Allow to cool, then chill until required.

**Soak** the rice noodles in cold water until soft. Chill
until required.

**When** ready to serve, reheat the coconut broth, add
the fennel and green beans and simmer for 5 minutes.
Tear half the coriander into pieces, add to the broth
with the drained noodles, corn cobs and prawns and
simmer for 4–5 minutes until piping hot. Ladle into
bowls and garnish with the remaining coriander.

**For chicken Thai green curry**, chop 8 boneless,
skinless chicken thighs into bite-sized pieces. Fry
the chicken with the onion paste, add 2 small sliced
carrots then the coconut broth ingredients and simmer
for 15 minutes until tender. Allow to cool and chill
until required. Reheat the curry and add the corn
cobs, noodles and coriander as above.

# minted pea & sesame falafel

Preparation time **25 minutes**
Finishing time **5 minutes**
Serves **4**

250 g (8 oz) frozen **peas**, just
  defrosted
2 x 400 g (13 oz) cans
  **chickpeas**, drained
1 **onion**, peeled and quartered
1½ teaspoons **cumin** seeds,
  roughly crushed
1½ teaspoons **coriander**
  seeds, roughly crushed
1 teaspoon ground **turmeric**
3 tablespoons chopped **mint**
2 tablespoons **sesame** seeds
1 tablespoon plain **flour**
3 tablespoons **olive oil**
**salt** and **pepper**

**Radish cacik**
200 g (7 oz) low-fat natural
  **yogurt**
100 g (3½ oz) **radishes**, finely
  diced
5 cm (2 inch) piece of
  **cucumber**, finely diced
2 tablespoons chopped **mint**

**Finely** chop the peas, chickpeas and onion together in a blender or food processor. Alternatively, chop them finely with a knife. Mix in the crushed seeds, turmeric, mint and seasoning.

**Spoon** 20 mounds of the mixture on to a baking sheet, then roll into ovals with the palms of your hands. Mix the sesame seeds and flour on a plate, then roll the falafel in the mixture and return to the baking sheet. Cover and chill until required.

**Mix** all the cacik ingredients together, season to taste and spoon into a serving bowl. Cover and chill until required.

**When** ready to serve, heat 2 tablespoons of the oil in a large frying pan, add the falafel and fry, turning, until golden brown and piping hot, adding the remaining oil if needed. Serve immediately with the cacik, a green salad and warmed pitta breads.

**For carrot & coriander falafel**, boil 250 g (8 oz) roughly chopped carrots until just tender and use instead of the peas. Substitute fresh coriander for the mint. Use diced cucumber and chopped coriander in the cacik instead of the radishes and mint.

# mixed mushroom straccatto

Preparation time **15 minutes**, plus soaking
Cooking time **25–30 minutes**
Finishing time **8–10 minutes**
Serves **4**

15 g (½ oz) dried **porcini** or mixed mushrooms
300 ml (½ pint) boiling **water**
1 tablespoon **olive oil**
1 **onion**, chopped
2 **garlic** cloves, finely chopped
300 g (10 oz) small chestnut **mushrooms**, halved or quartered
400 g (13 oz) can chopped **tomatoes**
½ teaspoon ground **cinnamon**
1 **bay** leaf
250 g (8 oz) **pasta** shells
**basil leaves**
**Parmesan** shavings
**salt** and **pepper**

**Soak** the dried mushrooms in the boiling water for 15 minutes. Meanwhile, heat the oil in a saucepan, add the onion and fry for 5 minutes, stirring until just beginning to brown. Stir in the garlic and fresh mushrooms and fry for 2–3 minutes. Add the tomatoes, cinnamon, bay leaf and seasoning.

**Add** the soaked mushrooms and soaking liquid, bring the mixture to the boil then cover and simmer gently for 20 minutes, stirring from time to time. Allow to cool and chill until required.

**When** ready to serve, cook the pasta in a large saucepan of boiling water for 8–10 minutes until just tender. Reheat the mushroom mixture, stirring until piping hot.

**Drain** the pasta, return to the pan and toss with the mushroom mixture. Spoon into shallow bowls and top with basil leaves and Parmesan shavings to serve.

**For mushroom straccatto puff pie**, spoon the mushroom mixture into a 1.2 litre (2 pint) pie dish and brush the top edge of the dish with water. Cut some narrow strips from a 200 g (7 oz) sheet of ready-rolled puff pastry and press on to the rim of the dish. Brush the strips with egg, then cover the dish with the remaining pastry and trim off the excess. Press the pastry edges together, flute and crimp. Bake in a preheated oven, 200°C (400°F), Gas Mark 6, for 30 minutes until well risen and golden.

# leek & chestnut patties

Preparation time **20 minutes**
Cooking time **15 minutes**
Finishing time **10 minutes**
Serves **4**

875 g (1¾ lb) **swede**, diced
3–4 tablespoons semi-
 skimmed **milk**
375 g (12 oz) **leeks**, finely
 chopped
50 g (2 oz) ready-to-eat pitted
 **prunes**, finely chopped
50 g (2 oz) **Brazil nuts**,
 roughly chopped
240 g (7½ oz) can whole
 peeled **chestnuts**, crumbled
125 g (4 oz) fresh
 **breadcrumbs**
1 **egg**, beaten
2–3 tablespoons sunflower **oil**
**salt** and **pepper**

**Cranberry sauce**
2 teaspoons **cornflour**
200 ml (7 fl oz) **vegetable
 stock**
2 tablespoons **cranberry
 sauce**
1 tablespoon red wine **vinegar**
1 teaspoon Dijon **mustard**
1 teaspoon **tomato purée**

**Cook** the swede in a saucepan of boiling water for 15 minutes until tender. Drain and mash the swede with the measured milk and some seasoning. Spoon into a microwave-proof bowl, allow to cool, cover with clingfilm and chill until required.

**Meanwhile**, mix together the leeks, prunes, Brazil nuts and chestnuts in a large bowl. Mix in the breadcrumbs, egg and seasoning. Shape into 16 patties, arrange on a baking sheet, cover loosely and chill until required.

**To** make the sauce, mix the cornflour with a little water in a small bowl until smooth. Put the vegetable stock, cranberry sauce, vinegar, mustard and tomato purée in a jug. Add the cornflour mixture, stir well and chill.

**When** ready to serve, heat 2 tablespoons of the oil in a frying pan, add the patties and fry over a medium heat for 10 minutes, turning several times until browned and hot through. Add the remaining oil if needed.

**Push** the patties to one side of the frying pan, add the sauce mix and bring to the boil, stirring until thickened. Meanwhile, reheat the swede in a microwave on full power for 2½–3 minutes until piping hot. Stir, then spoon on to serving plates and top with the patties and sauce.

**For turkey, leek & prune patties**, mix 1 chopped leek with 50 g (2 oz) ready-to-eat chopped prunes, 500 g (1 lb) minced turkey, 50 g (2 oz) fresh breadcrumbs, 1 egg yolk and seasoning. Shape into 20 small meatballs and chill until required. Fry in oil as above for 15 minutes. Make the sauce as above and serve with mashed potato instead of swede.

# sage & tomato pilaff

Preparation time **15 minutes**
Cooking time **40–45 minutes**
Finishing time **20 minutes**
Serves **4**

500 g (1 lb) plum **tomatoes**
1 **red pepper**, cored,
    deseeded and quartered
1 **onion**, roughly chopped
2 tablespoons **olive oil**
small bunch of **sage**
200 g (7 oz) easy-cook long-
    grain **white** and **wild rice**
    mixed
**salt** and **pepper**

**Cut** each tomato into 8 and thickly slice the pepper quarters. Place in a roasting tin with the onion, then drizzle with the oil and season well. Tear some of the sage into pieces and sprinkle over the vegetables. Roast in a preheated oven, 200°C (400°F), Gas Mark 6, for 40–45 minutes until softened.

**Meanwhile**, cook the rice in a saucepan of boiling water for 15 minutes until only just cooked. Drain, rinse in cold water and drain again well. Mix the rice into the cooked tomatoes and peppers, then cover with foil. Allow to cool and chill until required.

**When** ready to serve, reheat in a preheated oven, 180°C (350°F), Gas Mark 4, still covered with foil for 20 minutes until piping hot. Stir well then spoon into bowls and sprinkle with the remaining sage leaves. Serve with warm ciabatta or herb bread.

**For pumpkin & blue cheese pilaff**, roast 500 g (1 lb) peeled, deseeded and diced pumpkin (or butternut squash) with 3 halved plum tomatoes and onion as above. Cook the rice for 15 minutes then drain, allow to cool and then chill until required. Reheat as above, then top with 125 g (4 oz) crumbled St Agur or other blue cheese and serve.

# seared cod with olive butter

Preparation time **20 minutes**
Cooking time **10–12 minutes**
Serves **4**

150 g (5 oz) **sugar snap peas**
500 g (1 lb) **courgettes**,
　sliced diagonally
1 tablespoon **olive oil**
finely grated rind and juice of
　1 **lemon**
4 **cod** fillets, about 125 g
　(4 oz) each
50 g (2 oz) pitted mixed
　**olives**, roughly chopped
50 g (2 oz) **butter**
small bunch of **basil**, roughly
　torn
**salt** and **pepper**

**Put** the sugar snap peas and courgettes on a large piece of oiled foil, sprinkle with the lemon rind and plenty of seasoning then top with the fish. Drizzle with lemon juice and sprinkle with a little extra seasoning. Seal the edges of the foil to make an air-tight parcel. Chill until required.

**Beat** the olives with the butter and half the basil. Season with pepper, then spoon on to a piece of greaseproof paper. Wrap tightly and roll into a small log shape. Chill until required.

**When** ready to serve, put the fish parcel in a grill pan, open the foil and top the fish with 4 slices of olive butter. Cook under a preheated hot grill for 8–10 minutes until the fish is browned and flakes when pressed with a knife. Lift out the fish and cook the vegetables for a few minutes more, until just tender and lightly browned.

**Spoon** the vegetables on to serving plates and top with the fish fillets and any pan juices. Top with the remaining butter, cut into thin slices, and garnish with the remaining basil.

**For seared salmon with ginger butter**, arrange 4 salmon fillets on top of the sugar snap peas and courgettes. Top with 50 g (2 oz) butter mixed with 3 tablespoons chopped fresh coriander, 1 tablespoon finely chopped fresh root ginger and 1 finely chopped garlic clove. Cook as above.

food for
friends

# lamb with pomegranate couscous

Preparation time **40 minutes**,
plus chilling
Finishing time **20–35 minutes**
Serves **4**

1.25 kg (2½ lb) leg of **lamb**
1 large **pomegranate**
2 **garlic** cloves
small bunch of **mint**, torn
6 tablespoons **olive oil**
1 tablespoon runny **honey**
finely grated rind and juice of
  1 **lemon**
175 g (6 oz) **couscous**
50 g (2 oz) **sultanas**
75 g (3 oz) pitted **dates**,
  sliced
½ red **onion**, finely chopped
450 ml (¾ pint) boiling **water**
50 g (2 oz) **pistachio nuts**,
  cut into slivers
2 teaspoons **harissa** (optional)
**salt** and **pepper**

**Remove** the bone from the lamb, make a horizontal cut through the thickest part of the meat then open out so it is about 4 cm (1½ inch) thick. Place in a shallow non-metallic dish. Cut the pomegranate in half and scoop out the seeds. Place half the seeds in a pestle and mortar with the garlic then crush roughly. Mix with half the mint, half the oil, the honey and half the lemon rind and juice. Season and spoon over the lamb. Cover and chill for at least 3 hours.

**Put** the couscous into a microwave-proof serving bowl, add the dried fruit, onion, remaining lemon rind and juice, then pour over the boiling water. Allow to cool then cover with clingfilm and chill until required.

**When** ready to serve, transfer the lamb to a roasting tin with some of the marinade. Roast in a preheated oven, 220°C (425°F), Gas Mark 7, for 20–25 minutes for medium rare, or 30–35 minutes for well done. Lift out the lamb, add the remaining marinade to the hot pan and mix with the pan juices. Pour over the lamb, cover tightly with foil and leave to stand for 10 minutes.

**Add** the reserved pomegranate seeds and pistachios to the couscous. Mix the remaining oil with the harissa, if using, drizzle over the couscous then replace the clingfilm and microwave on full power for 1½–2 minutes until piping hot. Sprinkle the remaining mint over the top and fluff up with a fork. Spoon on to serving plates, top with thickly sliced lamb and drizzle with pan juices.

# vegetable moussaka

Preparation time **20 minutes**
Cooking time **15 minutes**
Finishing time **30–35 minutes**
Serves **4**

5 tablespoons **olive oil**
1 **onion**, chopped
2 **garlic** cloves, finely chopped
500 g (1 lb) **courgettes**, cut
 into chunks
250 g (8 oz) closed cup
 **mushrooms**, quartered
1 **red pepper**, cored, deseeded
 and cut into chunks
1 **orange pepper**, cored,
 deseeded and cut into chunks
2 x 400 g (13 oz) cans
 chopped **tomatoes**
2–3 **rosemary** stems, leaves
 stripped from stems
1 teaspoon caster **sugar**
2 **aubergines**, sliced,
 sprinkled with salt for
 15 minutes
3 **eggs**
300 g (10 oz) low-fat natural
 **yogurt**
large pinch of grated **nutmeg**
75 g (3 oz) **feta** cheese, grated
**salt** and **pepper**

**Heat** 1 tablespoon of the oil in a frying pan, add the onion and fry for 5 minutes, stirring until just beginning to brown. Add the garlic, courgettes, mushrooms and peppers and fry for 2–3 minutes.

**Stir** in the tomatoes, rosemary, sugar and seasoning, bring to the boil then cover and simmer for 15 minutes. Tip into a shallow ovenproof dish, leaving enough space to add the aubergines and topping.

**Rinse** and dry the aubergines. Heat 2 tablespoons of the oil in a clean frying pan and fry half the aubergine slices until softened and golden on both sides. Arrange, overlapping, on top of the tomato mixture. Repeat with remaining oil and aubergines. Allow to cool then chill until required.

**Stir** the eggs, yogurt, nutmeg and a little pepper together in a bowl, cover and chill until required.

**When** ready to serve, stir the yogurt mixture once more then pour over the aubergines. Sprinkle with the feta and bake in a preheated oven, 180°C (350°F), Gas Mark 4, for 30–35 minutes until piping hot. Spoon on to plates and serve with garlic bread and salad.

**For lamb moussaka**, dry-fry 500 g (1 lb) minced lamb with 1 chopped onion. Add 2 chopped garlic cloves then mix in a 400 g (13 oz) can tomatoes and 300 ml (½ pint) lamb stock. Flavour with 1 teaspoon ground cinnamon and a large pinch nutmeg. Cover and simmer for 40 minutes, stirring occasionally. Tip into a dish and cover with aubergines and yogurt mixture as above. Top with feta or the same weight of Cheddar cheese.

# marinated monkfish kebabs

Preparation time **15 minutes**,
plus chilling
Finishing time **10 minutes**
Serves **4**

1 **onion**, grated
2 **bay** leaves
2 large **rosemary** sprigs
2 **garlic** cloves, crushed
grated rind and juice of
1 **lemon**
2 tablespoons **olive oil**
625 g (1¼ lb) **monkfish**, cut
into cubes
**salt** and **pepper**

**Mint raita**
250 ml (8 fl oz) **natural yogurt**
20 g (¾ oz) **mint**, chopped
pinch of **cayenne pepper**

**Mix** together the onion, herbs, garlic, lemon rind and juice and olive oil. Season with salt and pepper and pour over the monkfish. Cover and chill for 1 hour or until required.

**To** make the mint raita, mix together the yogurt, mint and cayenne pepper. Cover and chill until required.

**When** ready to serve, remove the monkfish from the marinade and thread on to skewers. Place the fish under a preheated hot grill and cook for about 10 minutes, turning occasionally, until browned and cooked right through.

**Serve** the monkfish kebabs with a bulgar wheat salad and the mint raita.

**For marinated chicken kebabs**, slice 500 g (1 lb) boneless, skinless chicken breasts then marinate in the mixture above, using a small bunch torn basil leaves instead of the rosemary and bay. Heat a ridged frying pan until hot, then add the chicken and fry until browned on both sides and cooked through.

# mushrooms with gorgonzola

Preparation time **20 minutes**
Cooking time **10–15 minutes**
Finishing time **15 minutes**
Serves **4**

4 large flat field **mushrooms**
2 tablespoons **olive oil**
2 red **onions**, sliced
1 teaspoon caster **sugar**
2–3 **thyme** stems, leaves
  stripped from stems
2 tablespoons balsamic
  **vinegar**
4 **tomatoes**, deseeded and
  diced
65 g (2½ oz) **sun-dried
  tomatoes**, drained and
  sliced
100 g (3½ oz) **gorgonzola**
  cheese, diced
200 ml (7 fl oz) **crème fraîche**
100 g (31/2 oz) mixed
  **watercress**, baby **spinach**
  and **rocket** leaves
4 slices of **ciabatta**
**salt** and **pepper**

**Peel** the mushrooms, leaving the stalks intact, then place in an ovenproof dish. Heat the oil in a frying pan, add the onions and fry for 5 minutes until softened. Stir in the sugar and cook over a medium heat for 5–10 minutes until very soft and lightly caramelized.

**Stir** in the thyme leaves, balsamic vinegar, fresh and sun-dried tomatoes and some seasoning. Divide the mixture between the mushrooms then cover and chill until required.

**Put** two-thirds of the cheese in a small saucepan, add the crème fraîche and a little seasoning then cover and chill until required.

**When** ready to serve, remove the cover and bake the mushrooms in a preheated oven, 200°C (400°F), Gas Mark 6, for 15 minutes until piping hot. Warm the cheese and crème fraîche mixture, stirring until the cheese has melted. Add the salad leaves to the sauce and cook for 30 seconds.

**Toast** the bread and divide between 4 serving plates. Scoop the wilted leaves out of the sauce and on to the toast, then put the mushrooms on top of the leaves. Sprinkle with the remaining gorgonzola then drizzle the sauce around the edges of the plates.

**For mushrooms with goats' cheese**, halve 2 goats' cheeses, about 100 g (3½ oz) each, and place half on top of each tomato-topped mushroom. Season and sprinkle with a little extra thyme. Bake as above and serve on toasted ciabatta on a bed of risotto.

# plaice with applewood crust

Preparation time **20 minutes**
Finishing time **12–14 minutes**
Serves **4**

4 x 150 g (5 oz) **plaice fillets**
75 g (3 oz) dry white
  **breadcrumbs**
3 tablespoons chopped flat-
  leaf **parsley**
1 **garlic** clove, crushed
finely grated rind of ½ **lemon**
25 g (1 oz) **walnuts**, finely
  chopped
25 g (1 oz) **Applewood** or
  **Lancashire** cheese, finely
  grated
2 tablespoons seasoned **flour**
1 **egg**, beaten
25 g (1 oz) **butter**
1 tablespoon **olive oil**
**salt** and **pepper**

**Place** half the breadcrumbs in a blender or food processor with the chopped parsley and garlic and blend together until the breadcrumbs are slightly green. Mix these breadcrumbs into the remaining crumbs, together with the lemon rind, walnuts and cheese. Season with salt and pepper and mix together well.

**Sprinkle** a little seasoned flour over each plaice fillet, then dip the flesh side of each fillet into the beaten egg. Place the fillets, skin side down, on a baking sheet and sprinkle the breadcrumb mixture over the fish. Melt the butter with the olive oil and drizzle over the top. Cover and chill until required.

**When** ready to serve, remove the covering and cook the fish on the top shelf of a preheated oven, 200°C (400°F), Gas Mark 6, for 12–14 minutes, or until the crust is golden brown and the fish cooked through. Serve with wedges of lemon, fresh herbs, matchstick chips and a green salad.

**For mackerel with a chive crust**, tear 25 g (1 oz) ciabatta bread into small pieces and mix with the grated rind and juice of ½ lemon, 2 tablespoons chopped chives, and some salt and pepper. Place 4 mackerel fillets, skin side down, on a baking sheet lined with non-stick baking paper. Press the crumb mixture on top, drizzle with 1 tablespoon olive oil and chill until needed. Bake as above and serve with a mixed leaf salad.

# braised duck with cranberries

Preparation time **20 minutes**
Cooking time **1 hour**
  **20 minutes**
Finishing time **30 minutes**
Serves **4**

4 **duck** legs, about 200 g
  (7 oz) each
1 red **onion**, cut into wedges
2 tablespoons plain **flour**
600 ml (1 pint) **chicken stock**
100 g (3½ oz) fresh or frozen
  **cranberries**
1 **orange**, halved and sliced
6 **star anise**
2 tablespoons **soy sauce**
2 teaspoons **Thai fish sauce**
  (optional)
625 g (1¼ lb) **celeriac**, peeled
  and diced
375 g (12 oz) **potatoes**, cut
  into chunks
25 g (1 oz) **butter**
2–3 tablespoons **milk**
**salt** and **pepper**

**Heat** a large frying pan, add the duck legs and dry-fry until browned on both sides. Lift out and transfer to a shallow casserole dish. Pour off half the duck fat and then add the onion to the pan and fry for 5 minutes until softened.

**Stir** in the flour then gradually mix in the stock. Add the cranberries, orange slices and star anise, then the soy sauce and fish sauce, if using, and some pepper. Bring to the boil then pour over the duck. Cover and cook in a preheated oven, 180°C (350°F), Gas Mark 4, for 1¼ hours. Allow to cool and chill until required.

**Meanwhile**, cook the celeriac and potatoes in a saucepan of boiling water for 15 minutes or until tender. Drain and mash with the butter, milk and a little seasoning. Spoon into a microwave-proof serving dish and cover with clingfilm. Allow to cool, then chill until required.

**When** ready to serve, reheat the duck in the covered dish in a preheated oven, 190°C (375°F), Gas Mark 5, for 30 minutes, removing the cover after 15 minutes. Reheat the mash in the microwave on full power for 3–3½ minutes. Stir well, then spoon on to 4 serving plates, top with the duck and spoon the sauce and fruit around.

**For gingered duck with orange**, omit the cranberries and spices, instead adding 2 tablespoons finely chopped fresh root ginger, and replacing 200 ml (7 fl oz) of the stock with dry white wine.

# chickpea & potato tagine

Preparation time **15 minutes**
Cooking time **46 minutes**
Finishing time **10 minutes**
Serves **4**

2 tablespoons sunflower **oil**
2 **onions**, roughly chopped
1 teaspoon **smoked paprika**
1 teaspoon ground **turmeric**
2 teaspoons **cumin** seeds,
   roughly crushed
500 g (1 lb) **potatoes**,
   scrubbed and cubed
400 g (13 oz) can **chickpeas**,
   drained
400 g (13 oz) can **pinto
   beans**, drained
100 g (3½ oz) pickled
   **lemons**, drained and
   quartered
600 ml (1 pint) **vegetable
   stock**
small bunch of **coriander**
125 g (4 oz) **feta** cheese,
   crumbled (optional)
**salt** and **pepper**

**Heat** the oil in a saucepan, add the onion and fry for 5 minutes until lightly browned. Stir in the spices and cook for 1 minute. Mix in the potatoes and drained pulses and stir well.

**Add** the pickled lemons, stock and seasoning. Bring to the boil then reduce the heat, cover and simmer gently for 40 minutes until the potatoes are tender. Allow to cool, then chill until required.

**When** ready to serve, reheat the potato mixture on the hob, stirring occasionally and topping up with a little water if needed until piping hot. Spoon into shallow bowls and top with torn coriander leaves and feta cheese, if using. Serve with warmed pitta or flat Arab breads, if liked.

**For spiced lamb tagine**, fry the onion in the oil as above, adding 625 g (1¼ lb) diced lamb fillet. Stir in the spices then add 375 g (12 oz) potatoes, cubed, and a 400 g (13 oz) can of chickpeas. Omit the pinto beans and pickled lemons, adding a 400 g (13 oz) can of chopped tomatoes instead. Cover and simmer gently for 1 hour. Set aside and reheat when required. Serve the lamb tagine with couscous and top with torn coriander leaves.

# beef steaks with mozzarella

Preparation time **15 minutes**
Cooking time **20 minutes**
Finishing time **12–17 minutes**
Serves **4**

2 tablespoons **olive oil**
1 **onion**, finely chopped
1 **garlic** clove, crushed
1 **courgette**, diced
1 **yellow pepper**, cored,
   deseeded and diced
1 **aubergine**, diced
6 plum **tomatoes**, skinned and
   diced
10 **basil** leaves, chopped
2 tablespoons vegetable **oil**
4 **beef** steaks
**salt** and **pepper**
4 thick slices of **mozzarella**
   cheese

**Put** the olive oil into a shallow pan over a medium heat
and sauté the onion and garlic until golden and crispy.
Add the courgette, yellow pepper and aubergine, and
cook for 5–10 minutes until softened. Add the
tomatoes to the pan with a little salt and pepper, then
add the chopped basil. Allow the mixture to cool, then
cover and chill until required.

**Heat** the vegetable oil in the same pan over a medium
heat. Add the steaks and cook for about 2–4 minutes
on each side, or according to taste. Season and remove
from the pan.

**When** ready to serve, place the steaks on a baking
sheet. Top each one with a quarter of the vegetables
and a thick slice of mozzarella. Cook in a preheated
oven, 200°C (400°F), Gas Mark 6, for 10–15 minutes
until piping hot. Serve immediately.

**For peppered steaks with Stilton**, coat 4 steaks with
1½ teaspoons roughly crushed black peppercorns
and chill until required. Fry in oil as above until just
cooked, then transfer to a baking sheet. Sprinkle with
175 g (6 oz) diced Stilton cheese, then flash under a
preheated hot grill until the cheese has just melted.
Serve with a watercress salad and chips.

# poacher's pie

Preparation time **30 minutes**
Cooking time **1 hour
20 minutes**
Finishing time **45–50 minutes**
Serves **4**

15 g (½ oz) dried porcini
**mushrooms**
150 ml (¼ pint) boiling **water**
75 g (3 oz) **butter**
1 tablespoon **olive oil**
700 g (1 lb 7 oz) **venison**,
diced
1 **onion**, chopped
2 tablespoons plain **flour**
200 ml (7 fl oz) red **wine**
300 ml (½ pint) **lamb stock**
1 tablespoon **tomato purée**
2 tablespoons **redcurrant jelly**
750 g (1½ lb) **potatoes**
2 tablespoons **milk**
2–3 teaspoons hot
**horseradish** cream
3 tablespoons chopped
**chives**
**salt** and **pepper**

**Soak** the dried porcini in the boiling water in a small bowl for 15 minutes. Meanwhile, heat one-third of the butter and the oil in a flameproof casserole and add the venison, a few pieces at a time. Add the onion and fry over a high heat for 5 minutes, stirring until browned.

**Stir** in the flour then mix in the wine, stock, mushrooms and soaking liquid, tomato purée and redcurrant jelly. Season then bring to the boil and cover the dish. Bake in a preheated oven, 160°C (325°F), Gas Mark 3, for 1¼ hours.

**To** make the topping, cook the potatoes in boiling water for 15 minutes until tender. Drain and mash with half the remaining butter and the milk. Stir in the horseradish, to taste, the chives and a little seasoning. Spoon the venison mixture into a 1.5 litre (2½ pint) pie dish. Dot the potato over the top then cover and chill until required.

**When** ready to serve, remove the cover from the pie and dot the potato with the remaining butter. Stand the dish on a baking sheet then cook in a preheated oven, 190°C (375°F), Gas Mark 5, for 45–50 minutes until golden brown and piping hot. Serve with green beans.

**For venison cobbler**, rub 40 g (1½ oz) butter into 250 g (8 oz) self-raising flour. Add 125 g (4 oz) diced Stilton and season well. Set aside until required. Mix in 1 beaten egg and 4–5 tablespoons milk to make a soft dough. Roll out thickly, cut into 8 wedges, arrange on top of the venison and brush with egg. Bake at 200°C (400°F), Gas Mark 6, for 40 minutes until well risen and golden and the venison is piping hot.

# roasted trout with rocket pesto

Preparation time **30 minutes**
Finishing time **20–25 minutes**
Serves **4**

400 g (13 oz) can **haricot beans**, drained
250 g (8 oz) cherry **tomatoes**, halved
1 red **onion**, chopped
4 fresh **trout**, heads removed
**salt** and **pepper**

**Rocket pesto**
50 g (2 oz) **rocket**, plus extra to garnish
25 g (1 oz) **pine nuts**
40 g (1½ oz) **Parmesan** cheese, finely grated
8 tablespoons **olive oil**

**Tip** the beans into a large roasting tin, add the cherry tomatoes, onion and some seasoning and mix together. Slash each side of the trout two or three times with a knife. Tuck the bean mixture in between the slits.

**To** make the pesto, finely chop the rocket leaves and pine nuts and pound in a pestle and mortar. Alternatively, blitz in a blender or food processor. Mix with the Parmesan, oil and some seasoning. Spoon a little of the pesto into the cuts in the trout and the inside of the fish, then spoon the rest of the mixture into a small bowl. Cover both and chill until required.

**When** ready to serve, remove the cover and roast the trout in a preheated oven, 190°C (375°F), Gas Mark 5, for 20–25 minutes depending on their size. Test by pressing a knife into the centre of the trout through the body cavity: if the fish flakes evenly and is an even colour it is ready. Transfer to serving plates and serve with spoonfuls of pesto and extra rocket, if liked.

**For roasted lamb with rocket and mint pesto**, make up the bean salad as above, put into a roasting tin and top with 8 lamb chops. To make the pesto, use 25 g (1 oz) rocket leaves and 25 g (1 oz) mint leaves. Spoon a little of the pesto over the lamb, then chill until required. Cook as above for 25–30 minutes.

# baked salmon with pernod

Preparation time **20 minutes**
Finishing time **25 minutes**
Serves **4**

50 g (2 oz) **butter**
200 g (7 oz) **pak choi**
200 g (7 oz) **fine asparagus**
4 **salmon** fillets, about 150 g
(5 oz) each
4 cm (1½ inch) piece of fresh
root **ginger**, peeled and
finely chopped
8 tablespoons **Pernod** or
**Ricard**
**salt** and **pepper**

**Butter** 4 large pieces of foil. Separate the pak choi leaves and thickly slice the larger ones. Trim the asparagus and cut each stem into 2 or 3 pieces depending on length. Divide the vegetables between the pieces of foil and place a salmon fillet on top of each one.

**Divide** the remaining butter between the salmon fillets, sprinkle with the ginger and a little seasoning then drizzle with Pernod. Bring the foil up and over the salmon and seal well. Chill the parcels until required.

**When** ready to serve, cook the parcels on a baking sheet in a preheated oven, 180°C (350°F), Gas Mark 4, for 25 minutes. Unwrap one of the parcels and pierce the centre of the salmon. If it flakes easily and the flakes are all one colour they are ready, if not, cook for a few more minutes and then retest. Transfer the salmon and vegetables to shallow serving bowls and serve with plain boiled rice.

**For baked cod with white wine**, use 4 sliced tomatoes instead of the pak choi. Add the asparagus then top with 4 cod steaks. Top with butter, adding a small bunch of chopped basil instead of the ginger and dry white wine instead of the Pernod, and bake as above.

# parmesan-breaded lamb chops

Preparation time **15 minutes**
Finishing time **20 minutes**
Serves **4**

75 g (3 oz) plain **flour**
1 tablespoon **sesame** seeds
2 racks of French-trimmed
   **lamb**, about 625 g (1¼ lb)
   in total
50 g (2 oz) **Parmesan**
   cheese, freshly grated
50 g (2 oz) fresh
   **breadcrumbs**
2 **eggs**, beaten
**salt** and **pepper**

**Season** the flour with salt and pepper and mix in the sesame seeds. Dip the lamb into the seasoned flour, coating it evenly all over. Mix together the grated Parmesan and breadcrumbs and season with salt and pepper.

**Dip** the lamb first in the beaten egg and then in the Parmesan mixture and coat all over, pressing the crumbs on to the lamb. Chill until required.

**When** ready to serve, cook the lamb in a preheated oven, 200°C (400°C), Gas Mark 6, for 20–25 minutes. Cut the lamb into 4 pairs of cutlets and serve with lemon halves, new potatoes, carrot matchsticks, beans and parsley.

**For redcurrant & rosemary lamb chops**, mix 3 tablespoons redcurrant jelly, 4 teaspoons finely chopped rosemary leaves, 2 chopped garlic cloves and 1 teaspoon roughly crushed black peppercorns. Arrange the racks of lamb with the fat uppermost, and spread with the jelly mix. Chill until needed then roast as above.

# bacon & sun-dried tomato chicken

Preparation time **35 minutes**
Finishing time **30–35 minutes**
Serves **4**

750 g (1½ lb) **potatoes**,
   peeled and thinly sliced
1 **onion**, thinly sliced
2 **garlic** cloves, finely chopped
   (optional)
300 ml (½ pint) double **cream**
25 g (1 oz) **butter**
4 boneless, skinless **chicken**
   breasts, about 150 g (5 oz)
   each
50 g (2 oz) **sun-dried**
   **tomatoes** in oil, drained
8 large **sage** leaves
8 rashers of smoked streaky
   **bacon**
**salt** and **pepper**

**Blanch** the potatoes in a saucepan of boiling water for 4–5 minutes until almost cooked. Drain into a colander. Layer the potatoes in a buttered 1.2 litre (2 pint) ovenproof dish with the onions, garlic if using, and seasoning. Pour the cream over the top and dot with butter. Cover and chill until required.

**Make** a slit down the side of each chicken breast and enlarge the slit to make a pocket. Divide the sun-dried tomatoes between the pockets, adding a sage leaf to each. Press a sage leaf on the top of each breast and sprinkle with seasoning.

**Stretch** the rashers of bacon by pressing a large cook's knife along the length of each. Wrap one rasher around each breast, then wrap a second at a different angle to the first to make a crisscross pattern. Put the breasts into a roasting tin with the ends of the bacon tucked underneath. Cover and chill until required.

**When** ready to serve, remove the covers and bake the chicken and potatoes in a preheated oven, 200°C (400°F), Gas Mark 6, for 30–35 minutes, alternating oven positions once during cooking until the potatoes and bacon are golden. Test the chicken by pressing a small knife into the centre of the breast; juices will run clear when ready. Transfer to serving plates and serve with a rocket salad, if liked.

**For pancetta & blue cheese chicken**, stuff the chicken breasts with 125 g (4 oz) dolcelatte in place of the sun-dried tomatoes. Wrap in 8 rashers of pancetta instead of the bacon. Drizzle with 1 tablespoon olive oil and continue as above.

# crab & sweet potato cakes

Preparation time **10 minutes**
Cooking time **10 minutes**
Finishing time **10 minutes**
Serves **4**

500 g (1 lb) **sweet potatoes**
250 g (8 oz) King Edward
  **potatoes**
1 small **egg**, beaten
250 g (8 oz) white **crab meat**
½ teaspoon **paprika**
3 tablespoons plain **flour**
**oil**, for shallow-frying
**salt** and **pepper**

**Peel** both types of potatoes and cook in a saucepan of lightly salted boiling water for about 15 minutes or until soft when pierced with the tip of a knife. Drain well, return to the pan and roughly mash. Allow to cool.

**When** the potatoes are cold, add the beaten egg, season with salt and pepper and mix well. Add the crab meat and mix into the potato mash with the paprika and flour.

**With** floured hands, shape 2 tablespoons of the mixture into a flat cake. Repeat until all the mixture has been used, then chill the crab cakes until required.

**When** ready to serve, heat the oil in a large frying pan and fry 4 crab cakes at a time for 3–4 minutes, turning occasionally, until they are golden brown on all sides and heated through. Remove from the oil and drain well. Keep warm while cooking the rest of the crab cakes. Serve immediately with garlic mayonnaise and crisp salad leaves.

**For garlic mayonnaise** to serve as an accompaniment, place 2 crushed garlic cloves and 1 small red chilli, deseeded and chopped, in a blender or food processor. Add 1 egg yolk and 1 tablespoon white wine vinegar and process well. With the motor still running, slowly add 150 ml (¼ pint) olive oil in a thin stream. If this is added slowly enough, the egg mixture will gradually thicken into a mayonnaise.

# shallot tart tatin

Preparation time **25 minutes**
Cooking time **12 minutes**
Finishing time **25–30 minutes**
Serves **4**

500 g (1 lb) **shallots**, peeled
50 g (2 oz) **butter**
2 tablespoons light
   muscovado **sugar**
3 tablespoons cider **vinegar**
a few **thyme** sprigs
250 g (8 oz) **puff pastry**,
   defrosted if frozen
**flour**, for dusting
**salt** and **pepper**

**Cut** any large shallots in half. Melt the butter in a 20 cm (8 inch) frying pan. Add the shallots and fry over a medium heat for 5 minutes until just beginning to colour.

**Add** the sugar and fry for 5 more minutes or until caramelized, turning from time to time so that the shallots cook evenly. Add the vinegar, leaves from the thyme sprigs and some seasoning and cook for 2 minutes.

**If** your frying pan has a metal handle then leave the shallots to cool for 20 minutes in the pan, if not transfer to a heavy based 20 cm (8 inch) buttered round cake tin.

**Roll** out the pastry on a lightly floured surface and trim to a 20 cm (8 inch) circle. Arrange on top of the onions and tuck down the sides of the frying pan or cake tin. Cover and chill until required.

**When** ready to serve, remove the cover and bake in a preheated oven, 200°C (400°F), Gas Mark 6, for 25–30 minutes until the pastry is well risen and golden. Leave to stand for 5 minutes, then loosen the edges with a knife. Cover with a serving plate or chopping board and invert the pan or cake tin on to the plate then remove. Serve warm, cut into wedges with a green leaf salad.

**For shallot, apple & walnut tart tatin**, reduce the shallots to 375 g (12 oz) and add 1 dessert apple, cored, peeled and cut into 8 slices. Fry as above, adding 2 tablespoons walnut pieces with the sugar.

# tindori & green mango curry

Preparation time **20 minutes**
Cooking time **35 minutes**
Finishing time **5 minutes**
Serves **4**

125 g (4 oz) green **lentils**, rinsed
3 tablespoons vegetable **oil**
1 teaspoon ground **turmeric**
2 teaspoons **garam masala**
1 teaspoon **cumin** seeds
1 teaspoon **black onion** seeds
1 red **chilli**, finely chopped
1 green **chilli**, finely chopped
3 large **tomatoes**, chopped
250 g (8 oz) **tindori**, rinsed and trimmed
2 tablespoons soft brown **sugar**
1 tablespoon **tamarind paste**
150 ml (¼ pint) boiling **water**
1 small green **mango**
1 small red **onion**, finely chopped
handful of chopped **coriander**
**salt** and **pepper**

**Cook** the rinsed lentils in a saucepan of boiling water for 20 minutes until soft. Drain well.

**Meanwhile**, heat the oil in a large saucepan and fry the turmeric, garam masala, cumin seeds and black onion seeds for 1–2 minutes or until the spices are sizzling and the mustard seeds begin to pop.

**Add** the chopped chillies and the tomatoes together with the drained lentils and tindori. Cover the pan and simmer gently for 10 minutes, stirring occasionally. Mix the brown sugar and tamarind paste with the boiling water and add to the pan. Stir well and simmer for a further 5 minutes. Season to taste and allow to cool. Cover and chill until required.

**Shred** the mango finely and mix with the red onion and coriander leaves. Cover and chill until required.

**When** ready to serve, reheat the curry gently over a medium heat until piping hot. Top with the green mango and red onion mixture and serve with chapatis.

# classic paella

Preparation time **40 minutes**
Cooking time 1¼ **hours**
Finishing time **15 minutes**
Serves **6**

4 **garlic** cloves
small bunch of **mixed herbs**
150 ml (¼ pint) dry white **wine**
2 litres (3½ pints) hot **chicken
   stock** or water
1 kg (2 lb) fresh **mussels**,
   scrubbed
4 small **squid**, cleaned and
   sliced into rings
4 tablespoons **olive oil**
1 large **onion**, finely chopped
1 **red pepper**, cored,
   deseeded and chopped
4 large ripe **tomatoes**, skinned,
   deseeded and chopped
12 skinless, boneless **chicken**
   thighs, cut into bite-sized
   pieces
500 g (1 lb) paella **rice**
large pinch of **saffron** threads,
   crushed
125 g (4 oz) fresh or frozen
   **peas**
12 large raw peeled **prawns**
**salt** and **pepper**

**Slice** 2 garlic cloves and crush the rest. Put the slices in a large heavy-based pan with the herbs, wine, 150 ml (¼ pint) of the stock or water and season well. Add the mussels, cover the pan and bring to the boil. Simmer for 5 minutes until the mussels open. Remove the mussels, discard any which remain closed, and chill the remainder until required. Strain the liquid and reserve.

**Fry** the squid in half the oil for 5 minutes, stirring frequently. Add the onion, red pepper and crushed garlic and cook gently, stirring frequently, for 5 minutes until softened. Add the mussel cooking liquid and tomatoes and season. Bring to the boil, then simmer over a gentle heat, stirring, for 15–20 minutes until the mixture is thick. Transfer to a bowl.

**Sauté** the chicken in the remaining oil for 5 minutes. Add the rice and turn it in the oil for 3 minutes. Stir the squid mixture into the pan. Add about one-third of the remaining stock and saffron and bring to the boil, stirring constantly. Cover and simmer for 30 minutes. Add more stock as the rice becomes dry and stir frequently. When the chicken is cooked, the rice is tender but still firm and almost all the liquid has been absorbed, remove from the heat and allow to cool. Cover and chill until required.

**When** ready to serve, reheat the paella over a gentle heat. Check the seasoning and add the peas and prawns, simmer, stirring, for 5 minutes, adding a little more stock or water if required. Add the mussels, cover the pan and cook for 5 minutes or until the mussels are hot. Serve immediately.

# maple lamb with sweet potatoes

Preparation time **20 minutes**
Finishing time **30–45 minutes**
Serves **4**

1 kg (2 lb) **sweet potatoes**,
  peeled and cut into 2.5 cm
  (1 inch) cubes
2 **onions**, roughly chopped
3 teaspoons **fennel** seeds
pared rind and juice of 1 large
  **orange**
4 tablespoons **olive oil**
2 racks of **lamb**, about 500 g
  (1 lb) each
2 tablespoons **maple syrup**
**salt** and **pepper**

**Put** the potato cubes and onions into a large roasting tin then sprinkle with the fennel seeds and seasoning. Tuck the orange rind strips in among the potatoes and drizzle with the orange juice and oil.

**Make** a space in the potatoes for the lamb and put in a single layer with the fat uppermost. Season the fat, cover and chill until required.

**When** ready to serve, remove the cover and drizzle the lamb fat with the maple syrup. Roast in a preheated oven, 200°C (400°F), Gas Mark 6, for 20–25 minutes for medium rare or 30–35 minutes for well done. Cover with foil towards the end of cooking for well done lamb.

**Lift** the lamb out of the tin, wrap in foil and leave to stand for 10 minutes. Stir the potatoes and continue cooking for another 10 minutes until brown around the edges. Spoon on to serving plates, cut between the bones of the lamb and serve 3–4 cutlets per portion. Serve with steamed green beans, if liked.

**For honeyed lamb with rosemary leeks**, drizzle the lamb with 1 tablespoon honey instead of the maple syrup and roast on its own. Slice 500 g (1 lb) leeks, stir-fry with 2 tablespoons olive oil and a handful of finely chopped rosemary. Stir in 150 g (5 oz) frozen peas and 3 tablespoons crème fraîche. Serve the lamb and vegetables with new potatoes.

# parmesan soufflés with carrots

Preparation time **25 minutes**
Cooking time **25 minutes**
Finishing time **25–30 minutes**
Serves **4**

65 g (2½ oz) **butter**
75 g (3 oz) **Parmesan**
  cheese, finely grated
75 g (3 oz) **Cheddar** cheese,
  finely grated
50 g (2 oz) plain **flour**
300 ml (½ pint) semi-skimmed
  **milk**
1 teaspoon Dijon **mustard**
4 **eggs**, separated, plus 1
  extra **egg white**
**salt** and **cayenne pepper**

**Glazed carrots**
25 g (1 oz) **butter**
375 g (12 oz) baby **carrots**,
  halved lengthways
3 tablespoons **Marsala** or
  **sherry**
2 tablespoons chopped
  **chives**

**First** make the glazed carrots. Melt the butter in a frying pan, add the carrots, cover and fry gently for 15 minutes, shaking the pan from time to time. Add the Marsala or sherry, season well and cook for 10 minutes until tender. Allow to cool then chill until required.

**Meanwhile**, butter the insides of 4 soufflé dishes, about 10 cm (4 inches) in diameter and 6 cm (2½ inches) tall. Mix the cheeses together, add 1 tablespoon to each dish then tilt the dishes until the insides are coated with cheese.

**Melt** the remaining butter in a saucepan, stir in the flour and cook for 1 minute. Whisk in the milk and bring to the boil, whisking continuously until very thick and smooth. Take off the heat and mix in the remaining cheese, egg yolks, mustard, salt to taste and a large pinch of cayenne. Allow to cool for 10 minutes, then gradually whisk in the egg yolks. Cool.

**Whisk** the egg whites until stiff, then fold a large spoonful into the cooled cheese sauce. Add the remainder and gently fold in. Divide the mixture between the soufflé dishes then freeze (uncovered) in the coldest part of the freezer until required.

**When** ready to serve, wrap the dishes with folded non-stick baking paper that stands 4 cm (1.5 inches) above the dishes and tie with string (see page 8). Cook in a preheated oven, 180°C (350°F), Gas Mark 4, for 25–30 minutes until golden brown and risen. The edges should be set and the centre still soft. Reheat the carrots and sprinkle with the chives. Transfer the soufflé dishes to serving plates and spoon the carrots around them.

# kashmiri pumpkin curry

Preparation time **20 minutes**
Cooking time **20 minutes**
Finishing time **5 minutes**
Serves **4**

2 **onions**, quartered
2 **garlic** cloves
4 cm (1½ inch) piece of fresh
  root **ginger**, peeled and
  sliced
1 large red **chilli**, halved and
  deseeded
1 teaspoon **cumin** seeds,
  roughly crushed
1 teaspoon **coriander** seeds,
  roughly crushed
5 **cardamom** pods, crushed
1.4 kg (2¾ lb) **pumpkin**,
  deseeded and peeled
2 tablespoons sunflower **oil**
15 g (½ oz) **butter**
1 teaspoon ground **turmeric**
1 teaspoon **paprika**
1 **cinnamon** stick, halved
450 ml (¾ pint) **vegetable
  stock**
150 ml (¼ pint) double **cream**
50 g (2 oz) **pistachio nuts**,
  roughly chopped
small bunch of **coriander**, torn
**salt** and **pepper**

**Finely** chop the onion, garlic, ginger and chilli in a blender or food processor, or finely chop by hand, and mix with the crushed cumin, coriander and cardamom.

**Slice** the pumpkin into 2.5 cm (1 inch) wedges, then cut the wedges in half. Heat the oil and butter in a large frying pan, add the pumpkin pieces and fry for 5 minutes until lightly browned. Push the pumpkin to one side of the pan then add the onion mixture and fry until beginning to colour.

**Add** the turmeric, paprika and cinnamon, cook briefly then stir in the stock. Season and bring to the boil. Cover and simmer for 10 minutes until the pumpkin is almost cooked. Allow to cool, cover and chill until required.

**When** ready to serve, add half the cream, half the pistachios and half the coriander leaves. Reheat until piping hot. Drizzle with the remaining cream, and sprinkle with the remaining pistachios and coriander. Serve with naan breads and a tomato and onion salad.

**For kashmiri chicken curry**, cut 8 boneless skinless chicken thighs into large chunks and use instead of the pumpkin. Fry in the oil and butter, then simmer in the stock for 30 minutes. Reheat and finish as above.

# balsamic chicken with roots

Preparation time **20 minutes**
Cooking time **4–5 minutes**
Finishing time **40–45 minutes**
Serves **4**

4 **chicken** thighs, skinned
4 **chicken** drumsticks, skinned
3 tablespoons balsamic
   **vinegar**
3 tablespoons white **wine**
small bunch fresh **sage**
550 g (1 lb 2 oz) **potatoes**,
   scrubbed and cut into
   wedges
275 g (9 oz) **parsnips**, peeled
   and cut into wedges
275 g (9 oz) baby **carrots**,
   scrubbed and halved
   lengthways
2 small red **onions**, cut into
   wedges
4 tablespoons **olive oil**
**salt** and **pepper**

**Slash** each chicken piece 2 or 3 times with a small knife then put into a large plastic bag with the balsamic vinegar, wine, sage and some seasoning. Seal the bag well and chill for 3–4 hours or until required.

**Cook** the potatoes in a saucepan of boiling water for 4–5 minutes until almost tender, then drain well and tip into a large roasting tin. Add the parsnips, carrots and onion wedges, cover and set aside until required.

**When** ready to serve, tip the chicken and the marinade into the roasting tin. Drizzle the oil over the vegetables and sprinkle with a little seasoning. Roast in a preheated oven, 200°C (400°F), Gas Mark 6, for 40–45 minutes, turning the vegetables once or twice until golden and the juices run clear when the chicken is pierced with a small knife. Serve with a mixed leaf salad.

**For balsamic chicken with Mediterranean vegetables**, marinate the chicken in the same way, using 3 stems of rosemary instead of the sage. Use 500 g (1 lb) scrubbed new potatoes (no need to blanch), 500 g (1 lb) courgette wedges, 3 quartered and cored red peppers and 1 bulb of garlic, separated into cloves but not peeled. Place in a roasting tin, drizzle with oil and roast with the chicken as above.

186

# game pie

Preparation time **45 minutes**
Cooking time **1½ hours**
Finishing time **25–30 minutes**
Serves **4**

25 g (1 oz) **butter**
1 tablespoon **olive oil**
1 oven-ready **pheasant**, halved
1 oven-ready **pigeon**, halved
2 **rabbit** or **chicken** leg joints
1 large **onion**, roughly chopped
100 g (3½ oz) smoked streaky **bacon**, diced
2 tablespoons plain **flour**
200 ml (7 fl oz) red **wine**
400 ml (13 fl oz) **chicken stock**
2 tablespoons **redcurrant jelly**
1 teaspoon **juniper** or **allspice** berries, roughly crushed
1 **bouquet garni**
375 g (12 oz) ready-made **puff pastry**
**flour**, for dusting
beaten **egg**, for glazing
**salt** and **pepper**

**Heat** the butter and oil in a large frying pan then fry the game, in batches, until browned. Lift out and put into a large casserole dish. Add the onion and bacon to the frying pan and fry for 5 minutes, stirring until golden. Mix in the flour then stir in the wine, stock and redcurrant jelly. Add the berries, bouquet garni and seasoning, then bring to the boil. Tip the sauce over the game, cover and cook in a preheated oven, 160°C (325°F), Gas Mark 3, for 1¼ hours. Allow to cool.

**Lift** out the game and take the meat off the bone. Return to the sauce, discard the bouquet garni then spoon into a 1.2 litre (2 pint) pie dish.

**Roll** the pastry on a lightly floured surface until a little larger than the top of the pie dish. Cut 1 cm (½ inch) wide strips from the edges and stick on to the dish rim with beaten egg. Brush the pastry strips with egg and lay the sheet of pastry on top. Press down, trim off the excess then flute the edges. Cut leaves from reformed trimmings. Chill, uncovered, until required.

**When** ready to serve, brush the pie with beaten egg then cook in a preheated oven, 200°C (400°F), Gas Mark 6, for 25–30 minutes until golden and piping hot inside. Serve with steamed Brussels sprouts and braised red cabbage, if liked.

**For beef & mushroom pie**, fry 750 g (1½ lb) diced stewing beef and 150 g (5 oz) quartered mushrooms in the butter and oil. Mix with the fried onion and bacon, then the flour and stock. Continue as above but cook for 2 hours in the oven before making up the pie as above.

# seafood stew with gremolata

Preparation time **20 minutes**
Cooking time **30 minutes**
Finishing time **15 minutes**
Serves **4**

½ teaspoon **saffron** threads
2 tablespoons boiling **water**
3 tablespoons **olive oil**
1 **onion**, roughly chopped
2 yellow **peppers**, quartered,
    deseeded and thickly sliced
400 g (13 oz) can chopped
    **tomatoes**
150 ml (¼ pint) **fish stock**
200 ml (7 fl oz) dry white **wine**
2 tablespoons **sun-dried
    tomato paste**
400 g (13 oz) baby new
    **potatoes**, scrubbed
4 tablespoons roughly
    chopped flat-leaf **parsley**
finely grated rind of 1 **lemon**
1–2 **garlic** cloves, finely
    chopped
625 g (1¼ lb) **cod** loin, cut
    into large cubes
250 g (8 oz) mixed **shellfish**
    and **squid**
**salt** and **pepper**

**Put** the saffron into a small cup, cover with the boiling water and leave to soak.

**Heat** the oil in a flameproof casserole, add the onion and peppers and fry gently for 5 minutes until just beginning to brown. Stir in the tomatoes, fish stock and wine. Mix in the tomato paste and some seasoning, then add the potatoes and saffron with its soaking water. Bring to the boil then cover and simmer for 20 minutes until the potatoes are just tender. Allow to cool, cover and chill until required.

**To** make the gremolata, mix together the parsley, lemon rind and garlic, cover and chill until required.

**When** ready to serve, reheat the sauce then add the cod and seafood. Cover and simmer gently for 15 minutes until the cod is just tender. Be careful not to overcook or the cod will fall apart. Sprinkle with a little of the gremolata, then ladle into shallow bowls. Serve immediately with warm rustic bread, salad and the remaining gremolata for sprinkling.

**For cod stew with pesto**, add 4 teaspoons basil pesto to the sauce instead of the saffron. Use 275 g (9 oz) cooked peeled prawns instead of the mixed shellfish, and sprinkle the finished dish with chopped basil leaves instead of gremolata.

# puddings

# apricot fool with shortbread

Preparation time **30 minutes**
Cooking time **30–35 minutes**
Finishing time **5 minutes**
Serves **4**

10 **cardamom** pods, split
200 g (7 oz) ready-to-eat dried
  **apricots**
50 g (2 oz) caster **sugar**
300 ml (½ pint) **water**
150 ml (¼ pint) double **cream**
150 g (5 oz) carton ready-
  made **custard**

**Cardamom shortbread**
seeds from 10 **cardamom**
  pods, finely crushed
150 g (5 oz) plain **flour**
25 g (1 oz) **cornflour**
50 g (2 oz) caster **sugar**, plus
  extra for sprinkling
125 g (4 oz) **butter**, diced

**Put** the cardamom pods and seeds into a saucepan with the apricots, sugar and water. Bring to the boil then cover and simmer for 10 minutes until tender. Remove the cardamom pods, purée the apricot mixture and allow to cool.

**Meanwhile**, make the shortbread. Put the crushed cardamom seeds into the bowl of a food processor with the flours, sugar and butter and blitz until the mixture forms a ball. Alternatively, put the ingredients into a bowl and rub the butter in with your fingertips until the mixture resembles breadcrumbs. Squeeze the crumbs together to form a ball.

**Tip** the mixture into a 23 cm (9 inch) ungreased loose-bottomed flan tin and press into an even layer with your hands. Prick the surface and bake in a preheated oven, 160°C (325°F), Gas Mark 3, for 20–25 minutes until pale golden. Mark into thin wedges then sprinkle with a little sugar and leave to cool in the tin.

**Whip** the cream in a bowl until soft swirls form, then fold in the custard. Add the apricot purée and lightly swirl together until the mixture is marbled. Spoon into 4 glass tumblers. Cover and chill until required.

**When** ready to serve, put each tumbler on to a saucer and add 2 shortbread fingers.

**For summer berry fool with shortbread**, mix 375 g (12 oz) defrosted and puréed mixed frozen summer fruits into the custard and cream mixture and add 1 teaspoon lavender flowers. Serve with shortbreads made with 1 teaspoon dried lavender flowers instead of the cardamom seeds.

# chocolate & gingernut mousse

Preparation time **25 minutes**,
plus chilling
Cooking time **10 minutes**
Finishing time **5 minutes**
Serves **4**

200 g (7 oz) **dark chocolate**,
broken into pieces
3 tablespoons strong **coffee**
3 **eggs**, separated
150 g (5 oz) **gingernut
biscuits**
40 g (1½ oz) **butter**
4 tablespoons **crème fraîche**
sifted drinking **chocolate**

**Melt** the chocolate in a bowl set over a saucepan of simmering water. Stir in the coffee, then gradually mix in the egg yolks one at a time. Leave to cool slightly.

**Place** the biscuits in a plastic bag and crush with a rolling pin to make fine crumbs. Melt the butter in a small saucepan then stir in the crumbs. Line 4 150 ml (¼ pint) ramekin dishes with clingfilm so that the film overhangs the edges of the dishes. Divide half the crumbs between the bases of the dishes and press flat.

**Whisk** the egg whites until soft peaks, then stir a spoonful into the chocolate mixture to loosen it slightly. Fold in the remaining egg whites using a metal spoon. Pour the mousse mixture into the dishes, level the surfaces then sprinkle with the remaining crumbs. Chill for 4–5 hours or until set.

**When** ready to serve, lift the puddings out of the dishes using the clingfilm and then peel the clingfilm away. Top each pudding with a spoonful of crème fraîche and then decorate with a light dusting of drinking chocolate.

**For chocolate & orange mousses**, leave out the biscuit crumb mixture and flavour the chocolate mousse with 2 tablespoons orange juice and 2 tablespoons Grand Marnier or Cointreau instead of the coffee. Pour into small glasses, then top with crème fraîche and drinking chocolate as above.

# plum tarts with saffron custard

Preparation time **30 minutes**
Cooking time **12–15 minutes**
Finishing time **5 minutes**
(optional)
Serves **6**

200 g (7 oz) ready-rolled **puff pastry**
50 g (2 oz) **butter**, at room temperature
50 g (2 oz) caster **sugar**
50 g (2 oz) ground **almonds**
1 **egg yolk**
6 ripe red **plums**, about 300 g (10 oz), pitted and thickly sliced
sifted icing **sugar**

**Custard**
4 **egg yolks**
50 g (2 oz) caster **sugar**, plus a little extra for sprinkling
1 teaspoon **cornflour**
large pinch of **saffron** threads
300 ml (½ pint) semi-skimmed **milk**

**Cut** the pastry into 6 even rectangles. Knock up and flute the edges with a sharp knife then transfer to a lightly greased baking sheet. Prick the centres of the pastries.

**Cream** the butter and sugar together, then mix in the ground almonds and egg yolk. Divide the mixture between the pastry rectangles, then spread into a thin layer, leaving a border of pastry around the edges.

**Arrange** the plums on top of the almond mixture, then bake in a preheated oven, 200°C (400°F), Gas Mark 6, for 12–15 minutes until the pastry is well risen and golden. Loosen the bases of the tarts with a palette knife then allow to cool.

**To** make the custard, whisk the egg yolks, sugar, cornflour and saffron together in a bowl. Heat the milk in a saucepan until just boiling then gradually whisk into the egg yolks. Pour the milk mixture back into the pan then heat gently, stirring continuously, until almost boiling, and thickened and smooth. Tip back into the bowl and sprinkle with a little extra sugar to prevent a skin forming. Cover, allow to cool, then chill until required.

**Serve** the tarts and custard cold, or reheat if preferred and dust with a little sifted icing sugar.

**For mincemeat & apple tarts with orange custard**, top each rectangle of pastry with 1 tablespoon mincemeat, then add half a cored and sliced dessert apple. Bake as above and serve with custard flavoured with the grated rind of ½ small orange instead of the saffron.

# babacos & lime sorbet

Preparation time **15 minutes**, plus freezing
Cooking time **10 minutes**
Serves **4**

125 g (4 oz) granulated **sugar**
150 ml (¼ pint) **water**
500 g (1 lb) **babacos** or ripe **papaya**, deseeded, peeled and diced
finely grated rind and juice of 2 **limes**
**lime** wedges

**Put** the granulated sugar in a saucepan with the measured water and heat gently to dissolve the sugar. Increase the heat, bring to the boil and stop stirring. Boil for 5 minutes. Remove from the heat and allow to cool.

**Set** aside 2 tablespoons of diced fruit, and put the remainder in a food processor or blender with the cooled sugar syrup. Blend until smooth. Add the lime rind and juice to the purée and pour into a shallow metal container. Freeze for 3 hours.

**Remove** from the freezer and beat with a fork to break up the ice crystals. Stir in the reserved diced fruit, return to the freezer and freeze until solid.

**When** ready to serve, remove the sorbet from the freezer and allow to stand for 10 minutes. Scoop into small glasses and serve topped with a lime wedge.

**For raspberry sorbet**, make the syrup as above then allow to cool. Purée 500 g (1 lb) raspberries, sieve and mix with the syrup and the grated rind and juice of 1 lemon. Omit the chopped fruit and freeze as above. Serve with extra raspberries.

# coconut crème caramel

Preparation time **15 minutes**,
  plus chilling
Cooking time **30 minutes**
Serves **4**

125 g (4 oz) granulated **sugar**
125 ml (4 fl oz) **water**
2 tablespoons boiling **water**
2 **eggs**, plus 2 extra **egg
  yolks**
2 tablespoons caster **sugar**
400 ml (13 fl oz) can reduced-
  fat **coconut milk**
125 ml (4 fl oz) semi-skimmed
  **milk**
150 g (5 oz) **raspberries**

**Heat** the granulated sugar and water in a small saucepan, stirring occasionally, until the sugar has just dissolved. Bring to the boil and cook, without stirring, for 5 minutes until golden.

**Take** the pan off the heat, add the boiling water then stand well back, tilting the pan to mix, until the bubbles have subsided. Divide the caramel between 4, 250 ml (8 fl oz) metal pudding moulds, then swirl the caramel over the inside. Put the moulds in a roasting tin.

**Whisk** the eggs, egg yolks and caster sugar together to mix. Pour the coconut milk and semi-skimmed milk into a saucepan and bring just to the boil, then gradually whisk into the eggs. Strain into the moulds.

**Pour** hot (not boiling) water into the roasting tin to come halfway up the sides of the moulds. Cover the tops loosely with buttered foil then bake in a preheated oven, 160°C (325°F), Gas Mark 3, for 30 minutes until just set. Remove from the oven and leave the moulds in the water for 10 minutes. Lift them out, allow to cool then chill for 4 hours or longer until required.

**When** ready to serve, dip the bases of the moulds into boiling water for 10 seconds, loosen, then turn out on to rimmed serving plates. Decorate with raspberries.

**For chocolate custard pots**, whisk 2 eggs, 2 egg yolks and 50 g (2 oz) caster sugar together. Heat 150 ml (¼ pint) double cream and 450 ml (¾ pint) milk in a pan with 150 g (5 oz) dark chocolate, stirring until melted. Whisk into the eggs then pour into small heatproof dishes. Cook as above for 20–25 minutes. Cool and serve with cream.

# gingered treacle tart

Preparation time **30 minutes**
Cooking time **45–55 minutes**
Finishing time **15 minutes**
(optional)
Serves **8**

680 g (1 lb 6 oz) jar **golden syrup**
25 g (1 oz) **butter**
finely grated rind and juice of 1 **lemon**
125 g (4 oz) fresh **breadcrumbs**
50 g (2 oz) glacé or stem **ginger** drained and chopped
2 Braeburn **apples**, cored and coarsely grated
200 g (7 oz) plain **flour**
100 g (3½ oz) **butter**, diced
2 tablespoons cold **water**
1 tablespoon **milk**

**Tip** the golden syrup into a saucepan, add the butter and heat gently until melted. Stir in the lemon juice, breadcrumbs, ginger and apples then leave to cool.

**To** make the pastry, put the flour, butter and lemon rind into a bowl and rub in the butter until the mixture resembles fine breadcrumbs. Add the measured water and mix to a smooth dough, adding a little extra water if necessary. Knead lightly, roll out and use to line a 24 cm (9½ inch) loose-bottomed tart tin. Trim off the excess and reserve.

**Pour** the syrup mixture into the tart case. Roll out the pastry trimmings thinly, cut narrow strips and arrange in a lattice, sticking the edges with a little milk. Then glaze all of the strips with milk. Place the tart on a hot baking sheet then bake in a preheated oven, 190°C (375°F), Gas Mark 5, for 40–50 minutes until golden and the filling has set. Cover the top loosely with foil after 30 minutes, if necessary, to prevent the tart burning. Set aside until required.

**When** ready to serve, warm the tart in a preheated oven, 160°C (325°F), Gas Mark 3, for 15 minutes or serve cold with clotted cream or vanilla ice cream.

**For pecan pie**, make up the tart case as above. Warm 175 g (6 oz) golden syrup in a saucepan with 200 g (7 oz) light muscovado sugar and 75 g (3 oz) butter until melted. Cool slightly, then beat in 3 eggs and ½ teaspoon vanilla essence. Pour into the tart case and arrange 175 g (6 oz) of pecans on top. Bake at 180°C (350°F), Gas Mark 4, for 40–50 minutes until set, covering with foil if needed.

# persimmon & star anise jelly

Preparation time **15 minutes**
Cooking time **5 minutes**
Finishing time **5 minutes**
Serves **6**

600 ml (1 pint) **orange** or
  **mango juice**
1 **star anise**
75 g (3 oz) caster **sugar**
15 g (½ oz) **gelatine**
2 **persimmons**
75 g (3 oz) **blueberries**

**Measure** out 6 tablespoons of the orange or mango juice and set aside. Add the star anise to the remaining juice and the sugar in a saucepan and heat gently for 2–3 minutes, stirring frequently, until the sugar has dissolved. Remove from the heat and allow to stand until cold. Remove and discard the star anise.

**Put** the reserved orange or mango juice and the gelatine in a small bowl and leave to stand for 5 minutes. Heat over a pan of gently simmering water and leave until the gelatine has dissolved completely.

**Remove** the gelatine from the heat, leave to cool for 5 minutes and then stir it into the sweetened orange juice. Pour the mixture into a 600 ml (1 pint) loaf tin or jelly mould or into 6 individual jelly moulds. Chill for 20 minutes.

**Cut** the tops off the persimmons, peel back the skin and cut the flesh into small dice. Mix the persimmons with the blueberries and stir into the orange or mango jelly which will have begun to set. Return to the refrigerator and chill for 4 hours or until required.

**When** ready to serve, dip the mould or moulds into warm water to loosen the jelly, then turn out on to a plate. Serve topped with physalis, slices of persimmon and single cream, if liked.

# autumn berry crumble

Preparation time **10 minutes**
Cooking time **10 minutes**
Finishing time **20 minutes**
Serves **4**

300 g (10 oz) **cranberries**
150 g (5 oz) **blackberries**
150 g (5 oz) **blueberries**
4 tablespoons **water**
75 g (3 oz) caster **sugar**

**Crumble**
75 g (3 oz) fresh
  **breadcrumbs**
75 g (3 oz) ground **almonds**
75 g (3 oz) **butter**, diced
50 g (2 oz) caster **sugar**
25 g (1 oz) flaked **almonds**

**Put** the fruits into a saucepan with the measured water, cover and cook over a gentle heat for 10 minutes or until just tender. Stir in the sugar then tip into a shallow ovenproof dish, leaving room for the crumble. Allow to cool, then cover and chill until required.

**To** make the crumble, put the breadcrumbs, ground almonds, butter and sugar into a bowl and rub the butter in with your fingertips until the mixture resembles fine crumbs. Cover and chill until required.

**When** ready to serve, break up the crumble and sprinkle over the top of the fruit. Sprinkle with the flaked almonds, then bake in a preheated oven, 190°C (375°F), Gas Mark 5, for 20–25 minutes until crisp and golden. Cover with foil after 15 minutes if it is getting too brown. Spoon into bowls and serve with just-melting scoops of vanilla ice cream or hot vanilla custard.

**For apple & coconut crumble**, peel, core and slice 625 g (1¼ lb) cooking apples, and use instead of the berries. Use desiccated coconut in place of the ground almonds in the crumble and omit the flaked almonds.

# ricotta cake with summer fruits

Preparation time **25 minutes**
Cooking time **40–45 minutes**
Finishing time **5 minutes**
Serves **6**

175 g (6 oz) **ricotta** cheese
250 g (8 oz) caster **sugar**
125 g (4 oz) self-raising **flour**
100 g (3½ oz) **cornflour**
2 teaspoons **baking powder**
3 **eggs**, beaten
150 ml (¼ pint) light **olive oil**,
  or half virgin olive oil and half
  sunflower oil
2 tablespoons **Sambuca**,
  **sherry** or **kirsch**

**To finish**
2 **peaches**, halved, pitted and
  sliced
200 g (7 oz) **strawberries**
small bunch of seedless red
  **grapes**, halved
3 tablespoons **Sambuca**,
  **sherry** or **kirsch**
sifted icing **sugar**

**Mix** the ricotta and sugar together in a bowl. In a separate bowl, mix the flour, cornflour and baking powder together. Gradually whisk alternate spoonfuls of egg and flour into the ricotta until the mixture is smooth.

**Gradually** whisk in the oil in a thin steady trickle, then the liqueur or sherry to make a smooth thick batter. Pour the mixture into a greased and base-lined 23 cm (9 inch) springform cake tin. Level the surface then cook in a preheated oven, 180°C (350°C), Gas Mark 4, for 40–45 minutes until well risen and a skewer comes out clean when inserted into the centre of the cake. Allow to cool in the tin, cover and set aside until required.

**Mix** all the fruits together in a bowl then drizzle over the liqueur or sherry.

**When** ready to serve, loosen the edge of the cake, transfer to a chopping board and remove the lining paper and tin base. Dust heavily with sifted icing sugar and cut into thin wedges. Serve two per portion with a spoonful of the fruit and a little crème fraîche.

**For orange ricotta cake**, use Grand Marnier or Cointreau instead of the liqueur or sherry, adding 1 tablespoon finely grated orange rind to the cake. Serve with orange and blood orange segments drizzled with a little extra orange liqueur.

# lemon semi freddo with compôte

Preparation time **15 minutes**,
plus freezing
Cooking time **10 minutes**
Finishing time **5 minutes**
Serves **6**

600 ml (1 pint) double **cream**
175 g (6 oz) caster **sugar**
finely grated rind of 1 **lemon**,
plus juice of 2 lemons

**Blackberry compôte**
325 g (11 oz) **blackberries**
50 g (2 oz) caster **sugar**
4 tablespoons **water**
1 teaspoon **cornflour**

**Pour** the cream into a saucepan, add the sugar and heat gently, stirring, until the sugar has dissolved. Bring to the boil and cook for 1 minute then take off the heat, stir in the lemon rind and gradually mix in the strained juice. Pour into a deep non-metallic dish and allow to cool.

**To** make the compôte, put the blackberries, sugar and water into a small saucepan. Cover and cook gently for 4–5 minutes until the blackberries are just cooked. Mix the cornflour with a little water to make a smooth paste. Stir into the blackberries and bring back to the boil, stirring until the sauce has cleared and thickened. Cover and allow to cool.

**Freeze** the cooled lemon custard for 4–5 hours until just firm and partially frozen. Reheat the compôte. Scoop the semi freddo into small bowls or glass tumblers using a hot dessertspoon. Spoon the warm compôte over the top and serve immediately with biscotti biscuits.

**For chilled citrus pots with summer fruits**, add 125 ml (4 fl oz) mixed lemon, lime and orange juice to the sweetened cream and lemon rind mixture. Chill until set, then serve with mixed summer fruits. This dessert is not frozen.

# strawberry & vodka granita

Preparation time **30 minutes**,
plus freezing
Cooking time **3 minutes**
Finishing time **5 minutes**,
plus standing
Serves **6**

125 g (4 oz) caster **sugar**
300 ml (½ pint) **water**
500 g (1 lb) **strawberries**,
hulled, plus extra to decorate
4 tablespoons **lemon juice**
6 tablespoons **vodka**

**Tip** the sugar and water into a small saucepan, heat gently, stirring occasionally, until the sugar has dissolved then bring to the boil and cook for 1 minute.

**Purée** the strawberries in a blender or food processor until smooth then press through a sieve to remove the seeds. Stir into the sugar syrup with the lemon juice and vodka. Pour into a shallow container so that the syrup is no more than 2.5 cm (1 inch) deep, cover and allow to cool.

**Transfer** the dish to the freezer and freeze for 2 hours until just beginning to set around the edges of the dish. Break up the icy edges with a fork and return to the freezer. Beat with a fork every 30 minutes or so over a 2 hour period until the mixture has formed tiny ice crystals and looks like crushed ice. Freeze until required.

**When** ready to serve, remove the frozen granita from the freezer and leave at room temperature for 15–30 minutes until soft enough to mix. Spoon into tiny glasses set on small plates and decorate the plates with tiny halved strawberries, if liked. If feeling generous, drizzle with a little extra vodka.

**For orange & tequila granita**, omit the strawberries and add the juice of 6 oranges and 6 tablespoons tequila instead of the vodka.

# iced fig risotto

Preparation time **10 minutes**
Cooking time **40 minutes**
Finishing time **5 minutes**
Serves **4**

600 ml (1 pint) **milk**
40 g (1 ½ oz) caster **sugar**
finely grated rind of 1 **orange**
125 g (4 oz) risotto **rice**
8 fresh **figs**
**butter**, for greasing
2 tablespoons clear **honey**
2 tablespoons **orange juice**
200 g (7 oz) vanilla **ice cream**

**Put** the milk, sugar and orange rind in a large saucepan and bring almost to the boil. Add the rice and cook on the lowest possible heat, stirring frequently, for 25–35 minutes or until the rice is creamy but the grains are still firm. Remove from the heat and set aside to cool. Chill until required.

**Meanwhile**, halve the figs and place in a lightly buttered shallow ovenproof dish. Drizzle with the honey and orange juice and bake in a preheated oven, 200°C (400°F), Gas Mark 6, for 20 minutes, or until beginning to colour. Allow to cool, then chill until required.

**When** ready to serve, scoop the ice cream into the rice mixture and stir until it has just melted to make a creamy sauce. Spoon into bowls with the figs and cooking juices and garnish with thin slices of orange rind, if liked, and serve immediately.

# strawberry syllabub with brittle

Preparation time **20 minutes**
Cooking time **5–7 minutes**
Finishing time **1 minute**
Serves **6**

100 g (3½ oz) granulated
  **sugar**
3 tablespoons **water**
20 g (⅜ oz) flaked **almonds**
500 g (1 lb) **strawberries**,
  hulled
300 ml (½ pint) double **cream**
50 g (2 oz) caster **sugar**
finely grated rind and juice of
  ½ **lemon**
4 tablespoons white **wine**

**Put** the granulated sugar, water and almonds into a frying pan and heat gently, without stirring, for 2–3 minutes until the sugar has dissolved. Tilt the pan to mix the sugar, if needed. When dissolved, increase the heat and boil the mixture for 3–4 minutes until the syrup and nuts are just turning golden. Tip out on to an oiled baking sheet and allow to cool and harden.

**Meanwhile**, make the syllabub by puréeing the strawberries in a blender or food processor. Sieve out the seeds, if liked. Whip the cream until it forms soft peaks then whisk in the caster sugar, lemon rind and juice and wine. Fold in the strawberry purée and divide between 6 glasses, set on a plate. Chill until required.

**To** serve, lift the almond brittle off the baking sheet and break into shards. Arrange on the syllabub plate and serve immediately.

**For peach syllabub with brittle**, substitute sesame seeds for the flaked almonds in the brittle. Purée 3 pitted and sliced peaches, then press the purée through a sieve. Make the syllabub as above, using the peach purée instead of the strawberry purée.

# mini minted pineapple pavlovas

Preparation time **30 minutes**
Cooking time **about 1 hour**
Finishing time **10 minutes**
Serves **6**

**Meringues**
3 **egg whites**
175 g (6 oz) caster **sugar**
1 teaspoon **cornflour**
1 teaspoon white wine
  **vinegar**
½ teaspoon **vanilla essence**

**Filling**
4 fresh **pineapple** slices,
  peeled, cored and diced
2 tablespoons chopped **mint**,
  plus extra to decorate
2 tablespoons caster **sugar**
200 ml (7 fl oz) double **cream**

**To** make the meringues, whisk the egg whites in a large bowl until stiff then gradually whisk in the caster sugar, a teaspoonful at a time. Whisk for a minute or two more until the meringue is very thick and glossy.

**Mix** the cornflour, vinegar and vanilla together in a small dish then whisk into the meringue. Spoon the mixture into 6 mounds on a large baking sheet lined with non-stick baking paper and swirl into circles with the back of the spoon. Bake in a preheated oven, 110°C (225°F), Gas Mark ½, for 50–60 minutes or until the meringues can be easily peeled off the paper. Leave to cool on the baking tray.

**Meanwhile**, mix the pineapple in a bowl with the chopped mint and caster sugar. Cover and chill until required.

**When** ready to serve, whip the cream until softly peaking. Stir the pineapple and fold half the fruit and any juices into the cream. Transfer the pavlovas to serving plates, spoon the cream on top then spoon over the remaining pineapple. Decorate with mint leaves, if liked, and serve within 30 minutes.

**For strawberry & cassis pavlovas**, make the meringue bases as above. For the filling, mix 2 tablespoons caster sugar with 400 g (13 oz) sliced strawberries and 2 tablespoons cassis liqueur or elderflower cordial. Add half the strawberries to the cream as above, and top the pavlovas with the remaining strawberries.

# pistachio chocolate brownies

Preparation time **25 minutes**
Cooking time **25 minutes**
Finishing time **2–3 minutes**
Serves **6**

200 g (7 oz) dark **chocolate**,
  broken into pieces
200 g (7 oz) **butter**, diced
200 g (7 oz) light muscovado
  **sugar**
3 **eggs**
50 g (2 oz) plain **flour**
1 teaspoon **baking powder**
50 g (2 oz) **pistachio nuts**,
  roughly chopped

**Sauce**
100 g (3½ oz) dark **chocolate**,
  broken into pieces
150 ml (¼ pint) semi-skimmed
  **milk**
2 tablespoons light
  muscovado **sugar**

**Melt** the chocolate and butter in a large bowl set over a saucepan of gently simmering water. Whisk the sugar and eggs with an electric whisk until very thick and the whisk leaves a trail when lifted out of the mixture. Fold in the melted chocolate then the flour and baking powder.

**Pour** the mixture into a 20 cm (8 inch) square cake tin lined with non-stick baking paper and sprinkle with the pistachios. Bake in a preheated oven, 180°C (350°F), Gas Mark 4, for about 25 minutes until the top is crusty but the centre is still slightly soft. Allow to cool and harden in the tin.

**To** make the sauce, heat the chocolate, milk and sugar gently in a saucepan, stirring until smooth. Allow to cool, cover and chill until required.

**When** ready to serve, lift the brownies out of the tin using the paper. Cut into small squares, lift off the paper and transfer to serving plates. Add scoops of vanilla ice cream and serve with the reheated chocolate sauce.

**For white chocolate & cranberry blondies**, melt 200 g (7 oz) white chocolate, broken into pieces, with 125 g (4 oz) butter. Whisk 150 g (5 oz) caster sugar with 3 eggs as above then fold in the chocolate mixture. Fold in 150 g (5 oz) self-raising flour, and 50 g (2 oz) dried cranberries. Bake as above.

# banoffee cheesecake

Preparation time **30 minutes**,
plus chilling
Cooking time **about 1 hour**
Finishing time **10 minutes**
Serves **8**

250 g (8 oz) **digestive biscuits**
50 g (2 oz) **butter**
600 g (1 lb 3½ oz) full-fat **cream cheese**
75 g (3 oz) caster **sugar**
150 ml (¼ pint) double **cream**
4 **eggs**
2 ripe **bananas**, peeled
2 tablespoons **lemon juice**
125 g (4 oz) toffees, unwrapped
1 teaspoon **vanilla essence**

**To finish**
175 g (6 oz) **toffees**, unwrapped
150 ml (¼ pint) double **cream**

**Place** the biscuits in a plastic bag and crush using a rolling pin until they form fine crumbs. Melt the butter in a saucepan then stir in the crumbs and mix well. Tip the mixture into a greased 23 cm (9 inch) springform cake tin and press over the base and up the sides of the tin with the end of a rolling pin.

**Bake** the crust in a preheated oven, 180°C (350°F), Gas Mark 4, for 5 minutes then remove from the oven and allow to cool. Reduce the oven temperature to 150°F (300°F), Gas Mark 2.

**Beat** the cream cheese and sugar together in a bowl then gradually whisk in the cream then the eggs, one at a time. Mash the bananas on a plate with the lemon juice, crush the toffees, then stir into the cheese mixture with the vanilla essence.

**Pour** into the biscuit crust and bake for 50–60 minutes until the cheesecake is firm around the edges but still a little soft in the centre. Turn off the oven and open the door slightly. Leave the cheesecake to cool in the oven for 1 hour then take out and cool completely. Cover and chill for 4–5 hours or overnight until set firm.

**When** ready to serve, melt 125 g (4 oz) of the toffees in a small saucepan with 2 tablespoons of the cream. Loosen the edge of the cheesecake with a palette knife, remove the tin and transfer to a serving plate. Whip the rest of the cream and spread over the top of the cheesecake. Sprinkle with the rest of the toffees, smashed into pieces. Cut into wedges and serve drizzled with the warm toffee sauce.

# cidered apple jellies

Preparation time **20 minutes**,
 plus chilling
Cooking time **15 minutes**
Finishing time **5 minutes**
Serves **6**

1 kg (2 lb) cooking **apples**,
 peeled, cored and sliced
300 ml (½ pint) **cider**
150 ml (¼ pint) **water**, plus
 4 tablespoons
75 g (3 oz) caster **sugar**
finely grated rind of 2 **lemons**
4 teaspoons powdered
 **gelatine**
150 ml (¼ pint) double **cream**

**Put** the apples, cider, 150 ml (¼ pint) of water, sugar and the rind of one of the lemons into a saucepan. Cover and simmer for 15 minutes until the apples are soft.

**Meanwhile** put the 4 tablespoons of water into a small bowl and sprinkle over the gelatine, making sure that all the powder is absorbed by the water. Set aside.

**Add** the gelatine to the hot apples and stir until completely dissolved. Purée the apple mixture in a blender or food processor until smooth, then pour into 6 tea cups. Allow to cool then chill for 4–5 hours until fully set.

**When** ready to serve, whip the cream until it forms soft peaks. Spoon over the jellies and sprinkle with the remaining lemon rind.

**For cidered apple granita**, omit the gelatine and pour the puréed apple mixture into a shallow dish so that the mixture is about 2.5 cm (1 inch) deep or less. Freeze for about 2 hours until mushy around the edges, then beat with a fork. Freeze for 2 hours more, beating the granita at 30 minute intervals until the texture of crushed ice. Freeze until ready to serve, then scoop into small glasses.

# panna cotta with strawberries

Preparation time **20 minutes**,
  plus chilling
Cooking time **3–4 minutes**
Finishing time **5 minutes**
Serves **6**

3 teaspoons powdered
  **gelatine**
3 tablespoons cold **water**
1 **vanilla pod**
450 ml (¾ pint) double **cream**
150 ml (¼ pint) full-fat **milk**
65 g (2½ oz) icing **sugar**
400 g (13 oz) **strawberries**,
  roughly chopped
3 tablespoons **Pimms**
  (optional)
**mint** leaves

**Sprinkle** the gelatine over the cold water in a small bowl and set aside for 5 minutes. Meanwhile, slit the vanilla pod along its length and scrape out the seeds with a small knife, add to a saucepan with the pod, cream, milk and 50 g (2 oz) of the icing sugar.

**Bring** the cream mixture to the boil, add the gelatine, take off the heat and stir until the gelatine has completely dissolved. Leave to cool for 20 minutes, stirring from time to time so that a skin doesn't form. Remove the vanilla pod and discard. Divide the vanilla cream between six 150 ml (5 fl oz) individual metal pudding moulds. Allow to cool, then chill for 4–5 hours until set.

**Mix** the strawberries with the remaining sugar and the Pimms, if using. Cover and chill until required.

**When** ready to serve, dip the bases of the moulds into hot water for 10 seconds, then loosen the top edge, invert on to a small plate and jerk to release dessert. Lift off the mould and spoon strawberries around the dessert. Serve decorated with mint leaves.

**For strawberry panna cotta with summer berries**, omit 150 ml (¼ pint) of the cream and add 200 g (7 oz) puréed strawberries instead. Serve with 400 g (13 oz) mixed summer berries sweetened with a little sugar.

# chocolate & cardamom pots

Preparation time **10 minutes**
Cooking time **8 minutes**
Finishing time **5 minutes**
Serves **4**

200 g (7 oz) good-quality dark
  **chocolate**, broken into
  squares
seeds from 8–10 **cardamom
  pods**, crushed
2 tablespoons **coffee liqueur**
2 tablespoons extra virgin
  **olive oil**
3 large **eggs**, separated
4 tablespoons whipped
  double **cream**
sifted **cocoa powder**

**Place** the chocolate squares in a small, heatproof bowl with the crushed cardamom, coffee liqueur and olive oil and set over a pan of barely simmering water. Leave the chocolate to melt very slowly without stirring for about 8 minutes.

**Remove** the bowl of chocolate from the heat and quickly beat in the egg yolks. Set aside while you put the egg whites in a large bowl and whisk until stiff. Stir 1 tablespoon of the beaten whites into the chocolate mixture to slacken it, then carefully fold in the remaining egg whites with a metal spoon.

**Divide** the mixture between 4 ramekins or pretty coffee cups. Cover and chill for 2 hours, or until required. Serve with a little whipped cream and a dusting of cocoa powder.

**For chocolate brandy pots**, omit the cardamom pods and add 2 tablespoons brandy instead of the coffee liqueur. Decorate with chocolate coffee beans.

# sweet cheese with berries

Preparation time **25 minutes**
Cooking time **10 minutes**
Finishing time **5 minutes**
Serves **4**

50 g (2 oz) caster **sugar**
3 tablespoons **water**
2–3 fresh **lavender** heads
  (optional)
1 **egg white**
500 g (1 lb) **Quark** (soft
  cheese)
175 g (6 oz) **crème fraîche**

**Fruit syrup:**
25 g (1 oz) caster **sugar**
2 tablespoons **water**
250 g (8 oz) mixed **soft fruit,**
  such as raspberries,
  blueberries and blackberries

**Put** the caster sugar and water in a small saucepan and simmer gently until the sugar has dissolved. Add the lavender flowers to the syrup, if using, and simmer for 3 minutes. Remove from the heat and leave to cool.

**Whisk** the egg white in a clean bowl until it stands in stiff peaks. Mix the Quark and crème fraîche in another bowl, stir in the cold strained lavender syrup, then fold in the whisked egg white.

**Line** 4 perforated moulds or recycled, clean yogurt pots with small holes in the bottom, with damp pieces of muslin and stand the moulds on a plate to catch the liquid that will drip out. Spoon the cheese mixture into the moulds, level, and chill overnight or until required.

**To** make the fruit syrup, put the caster sugar and water in a small saucepan and heat gently to dissolve the sugar. Add half the fruit to the warm syrup and cook for 1 minute, then remove from the heat. When the syrup and fruit are cold, stir in the remaining fruit. Cover and chill until required.

**When** ready to serve, turn the cheeses out of their moulds on to 4 serving plates. Serve with the soft fruits and decorate with mint sprigs.

**For quick berry brulées**, divide 150 g (5 oz) raspberries and 100 g (3½ oz) blueberries between six 150 ml (¼ pint) heatproof dishes. Mix 200 g (7 oz) crème fraîche with 200 g (7 oz) natural yogurt, 2 tablespoons caster sugar and 1 teaspoon vanilla extract. Spoon over the berries. Refrigerate until ready to serve, then sprinkle each dish with 2 teaspoons caster sugar. Grill until golden.

# index

237

# acknowledgements

**Executive Editor:** Nicky Hill
**Senior Editor:** Charlotte Macey
**Executive Art Editor:** Penny Stock
**Designer:** Joanna Macgregor
**Photographer:** William Shaw
**Home Economist:** Sara Lewis
**Prop Stylist:** Liz Hippisley
**Senior Production Controller:** Martin Croshaw

**Special photography:** © Octopus Publishing
Group Limited/William Shaw
All other photography: © Octopus Publishing Group
Limited.